Half-off Sail
A Sea Story

By

Robert W. Fuller

"Success is never found.
Failure is never fatal.
Courage is the only thing."

Winston Churchill

Half- off Sail

Published: November, 2014

© 2014 Robert W Fuller. All rights reserved.

Published by: Ally Publishing Group, Sugar Grove, IL 60554
Please forward comments and suggestions to:
 AllyPublishingGroup@AllyBusiness.com

Printed in the United States of America. No part of this work may be reproduced or transmitted in any form or by any means, electronic, manual, photocopying, recording, or by any information storage and retrieval system, without prior written permission of the publisher.

ISBN-10: 1-940441-10-2
ISBN-13: 978-1-940441-10-8

FOREWORD

Insanity, pure and simple! It's the only explanation for what these two people did. Einstein described insanity as "doing the same over and over again and expecting different results". Well, he never met these two people. We can't blame it on stupidity. This is a story about a college professor and his graduate student. We can't blame it on lack of luck or equipment. The only possible answer is: insanity.

This is the story of a friend of mine, Bob Fuller: an intelligent, well-spoken and honest man. A person I love, respect and honor, but one with obvious flaws. I'm the consummate project manager and as such, I'm an expert in project risk management. Apparently, Bob hasn't taken any of my seminars on risk management.

Any experienced project manager will tell you: some projects go very smoothly; some projects have a few problems and some projects are just amassed with problems. You can recognize the latter right from the start. The problems start early and never let up. When you discover you're in one of these projects, it's wise to become very conservative very quickly. Certainly, you don't engage in any dangerous endeavors. Well, while *you* might avoid danger, this thought never seemed to occur to Bob.

The tale starts off simple enough: two people become friends and began looking for some interesting activities they can share. The activities are simple and relatively risk-free. Yet, even the simplest of these actions can yield disastrous results. As any sane and intelligent risk manager will attest, problems can quickly compound resulting in a catastrophe. One or two of these might not dissuade you from your goals, but disaster after disaster after disaster after disaster? Well, you get the picture.

So, even if we remove the extensive series of problems and even if we take away the universe's obvious omens and portents of disasters, you'll get to a point in this book and wonder, "what were they thinking?" Sailing, while not particularly dangerous, is not without risk. But what these two decided to do can only be described as insane.

Fortunately, I'm more than a project manager, I'm also a human being. While I am passionate about my chosen profession, I also recognize it has its own challenges. This is not a tale about project management. This is not a tale about risk management. This is a tale about friendship, mutual trust, the human spirit and its resilience in the face of disaster after disaster.

As the old saying goes, "Damn the torpedoes, full speed ahead!"

Enjoy,
Michael B. Bender
Author: "A Manager's Guide to Project Management"

PREFACE

Most people tender fantasies about the sea. They either want to live near it, swim in it, boat on it, eat from it or just watch it. The ever changing sea: beautiful, frightening, soothing but always engaging. It touches everyone. It seems like a workshop for fantasy. Generally, the fantasies are filed under dreams, and dreams are rarely acted upon. Something always seems to prevent dreams from coming true; not enough money, time, fear, too much reality.

This is a story of a dream becoming a reality. It takes place over a one year period in the late 1970's. It was a time when there were no cell phones, internet or GPS. It was the last years before everything related to connecting to others changed. It starts from a chance meeting in a classroom that leads two would-be adventurers on an ambitious a bike trip that ended in failure. That failure led to new adventures; a paddlewheel boat, and then to a sailboat. It recounts the time spent learning to sail from scratch to sailing a newly purchased boat to the Bahamas for the voyage of a lifetime. It Along the way we recount the loss of friends, hours of frustration, our first night on the open sea straight into an overnight storm being lost and adrift without an engine and turning back before eventually trying to cross from Florida to the Bahamas. It turns into the success of a second crossing, the joy of sailing, learning to spear fish for food, sapphire days and diamond nights among the island and the people.

It is a story for anyone that ever wanted to buy a boat and live a dream in distant harbors but never did. All of this occurred from a chance meeting with Dave Hopkins, my professor. Without him, all this would never have happen. With him, all that follows is a story that is hard to believe ever *did* happen.

DEDICATION

For my wife, Candy, and our two daughters Devon and Kyrin, for whom all my love and efforts are dedicated.

SPECIAL THANKS

This book would never have happened without the help of: Michael Bender, Kimi Ziemski, Norma Owen, Barbara Taylor, Betty Palmerton, Candy Fuller, Katherine Sturak, Becky Frolik, Jeffrey Scott Pearson, Gordon Joost and Mary Zlobl.

CONTENTS

Pedals to Paddlewheels 1

Paddlewheels To Sails 19

Learning to Sail 27

Practice Runs and Construction 45

Preparation 53

Night Of Terror 63

Broken Parts and Broken Hearts 91

The Second Crossing 105

Westend And Beyond 111

Play Time in the Shallows 129

The Huntsmen 141

Walkers Cay to Westend 147

PEDALS TO PADDLEWHEELS

The Indian Summer rain had me tearing at my necktie as I stepped from the Suburban Transit bus to the steaming pavement in Hightstown, New Jersey. I had left work in New York City early to make the evening class at Rider University, the second to last course I would have to take to complete my Master's degree in Business Administration. The irony of being so close to completing a master's degree hit me as I slid into the bucket seat of my '67 robin's egg blue VW bug. I hated school. And here, at 30-years old, I was completing my second master's degree. Somehow, after my sophomore year in college, I had begun to do better in school, working hard to overcome years of being a poor student. But if anyone would have told me that I would get out of college with a reasonable grade point average I would have challenged who they were really talking about, it couldn't have been me.

Down shifting I eased off Route 95 for the Lawrenceville exit. It was a 25-minute drive from the bus stop near my house in East Windsor, through the flat Princeton farmland, past countless track houses to the college. I wheeled on to the campus grounds at 6:15 p.m.

I drove to the back parking lot to be as close as possible to the Chapel where the course in Communication 451 was to be held. Skipping several steps on my way to the basement, I zipped around the various corridors looking for the room. By following the noise, I found the class already half assembled.

In general, it was a good group that made up the Rider program. Nearly all were working and had returned to school for a "practical" degree. The genius behind the development of this program was a living legend—Ray Male. Mr. Male, now the Associate Professor of Political Science and Program Director, had forced the University (then referred to as Rider College, a land grant agriculture school founded in 1860) administration to take on a business program that proved to be so popular that the highly regarded MBA program, also at the University, was beginning to suffer in enrollment. The students loved and supported the faculty of the Male program without question and endured the little games administration played that made signing up half the challenge. One such game was having classes in the Chapel basement, an odd place most agreed. Doctor Dave Hopkins, a new professor with the program, a Ph.D., from The Wharton School of Business and former AT&T exec., was in the basement waiting for his first class nonplussed. At first glance, he was an odd looking instructor resembling a cross between an Aspen ski instructor and David Soul. Blue eyes, a mustache, sandy blond hair, thinning ever so slightly (an observation students left unmentioned) and physically fit, his open neck plaid shirt was tucked neatly into his flared corduroy tan pants which suggested Colorado lineage. He was, in fact, from Ohio, but spent most of his life in Denver and clearly identified himself with that part of the country. His casual appearance was, we all were to learn, rather deceiving. He was a perfectionist as most "doctors" are, precise in language and thought and excuse intolerant. Yet he was also friendly, someone you treated with deference because that's the way he treated you. At least that's the way it appeared on the first night.

"Ok, let's get this class underway," Professor Hopkins said as the second hand swept past 6:30p.m. "What I want you to do is bring your chairs into the form of a circle." Quick glances gave way to chairs being dragged across the linoleum floor as we all circled up.

I gave a knowing nod to Ed Higgins, a partner in academia.

"Bet this is going be one of those touchy-feely classes." Ed chuckled under his breath smug in the knowledge that he would have an easy time in this course. Ed was a reporter for the Trenton Times, spoke fluent German, and had been a language specialist in the U.S. Army. He was an excellent communicator and had a George Carlin sense of humor, which made him the star debater at the pub after classes. For him to even take a course in communications smacked of the absurd. But, since it was an easy A, he obviously planned to enjoy himself and entertain the class as well. Dr. Hopkins had different thoughts.

"This is a course in communications. In the next several weeks we will learn the art of presenting ourselves with clarity and quality. When you open your mouth, I want you to say something of note. I will cut you off whenever you just talk for the sake of talking. Talkers entertain mindless listeners only."

Dr. Hopkins paused and looked around the room. There was a smile on his face, but there was also a wrinkle in his brow indicating he was somewhat serious about all this. And if the professor is serious, wise students know they'd better get serious too.

"For openers, I want each of you to introduce yourselves. Say something we can remember about you, something that is better than 'I was born in July' - Ok, let's see. Robin, you start."

Robin, a red-haired minx, blanched. "I.... uh.... well.... damn it! Why did you have to start with me?"

"Good Robin. Good start." The class burst out laughing. "You hotshots can talk a blue streak over there at the pub, but in a serious conversation it's difficult to say something poignant, positive and memorable about yourselves. Now, try it again. Craig, you're on."

Although it was a relief knowing I was not next, I was beginning a quick mental search of my past for something that would be positive and memorable. I was not alone. Everyone now had that slightly panicked look on their face. It was a group of bright, articulate people who hated to sound stupid, but here we were sounding as stupid as a stockbroker predicting the future.

"Well, hello, my name is Craig, which, uh.... you just heard, (laughter) and, I uh, like to play the guitar. I also..." Craig was not doing much better, and Dr. Hopkins cut him off.

"Thank you Craig. Now come on gals and guys. I am talking about impact. Give us some power, something valuable to listen to. Engage us. Make us want to hear more."

This was getting serious. If our name and hobby did not seem to be the right opener, then something else was needed, something very provocative. Dr. Hopkins looked around the room. Almost everyone's eyes darted to the floor. He picked up the roster and flashed down the list of names, and landed on the one I least wanted to hear....mine.

"Fuller, let's hear from you. Remember. Something important."

With a slight pause, I opened with my best shot.
"A powerful moment in my 30-year life was the exhausted joy I felt riding my bicycle into Washington, D.C. after crossing the country in 40 days at 16-years-old." I paused only long enough to let that sink in and began again. "The years that followed...."

"Hold it! Are you serious about the bike trip across the country?" Dr. Hopkins said, standing up. He began slowly walking over to the long table against the hallway wall and sat down, one foot off the floor, and leaned forward with a look of real interest. A small ripple of relief gurgled up from within. I thought, "I just may have passed the first hurdle."

"Yeah... why?" I responded.

"It's impressive, that's why." Dr. Hopkins added something about seeing him after class, turned to the class and began to *professorialize* the experience. He assured those not interested in cycling that there were more ways to grab attention, to compel people to hear more. The exercise continued with renewed interest, and I settled back to watch the fun.

Whatever else was said drifted past me as I wondered what Dr. Hopkins' wanted to talk about after class. When class finally did end 2½ hours later, he stopped me at the door.

"Fuller, stick around a minute." he said, then finished up with the usual questions students ask teachers after class to draw attention to themselves. As the last student left he collected his papers, rammed them into his leather case and motioned me to the door as he hit the light switch.

The air was considerably cooler at 9 p.m. We began walking and talking across the quad toward the commons, interrupted only by occasional passing acquaintances.

"I have to attend a faculty party. No big thing, just wine and cheese. Why don't you join me and we can talk about that bike trip of yours after we make the social rounds?"

"Did you say wine? Sure, I think I can squeeze in that kind of faculty party."

He smiled and we were at ease with one another from the first step. In another few minutes we were climbing the stairs to the second story faculty lounge and weaving our way toward the wine and cheese.

Through the cloud of smoke, the smell of feta, the taste of Chardonnay and din of conversation, Dr. Hopkins and I were finally able to find two unoccupied seats off in the corner. We spent several more minutes wolfing down the fancy cheese and a few glasses of wine. Setting down his third glass of wine, Dr. Hopkins nodded to a few passing faces and turned to me. "Now, tell me about this bike trip of yours."

Dr. Hopkins apparently had no intention of talking about the class. He was clearly interested in biking and my trip was more than a good story. I wove my attentive listener through the deserts of California, Arizona, to the high desert of New Mexico, into a hospital for an infected toe in Santa Fe, up the five-mile hike through Raton Pass in Colorado, a day of rest at the Air Force Academy, then on across the flat lands of Kansas and its dust bowl of head winds. After 20 days, we reached the mighty Missouri, crossed at Hannibal, and cycled on through the cornfields of Pennsylvania, down through washboard mountains of West Virginia to Maryland. Finally, 40-days later, (30 riding, 10 resting) we cycled into Washington, D.C. itself. We were supposed to meet

President Kennedy because of his big push on physical fitness but, sadly, his newborn son Patrick died two days after we arrived and we missed an opportunity for a photo and hand shake. That would have been some photo in light of the events that followed in Dallas three months later in 1963. "I've a thousand questions but first, let's get some more wine" he said, dragging me out of the deep cushioned chair. He poured and asked a string of technical details at the same time. When we returned to our chairs, he announced what was *really* had been on his mind throughout my entire monologue. "How would you like to try that trip again?"

"Me? I think I'm a little out of shape now for that sort of thing. But through the two glasses of wine, there was something in me that really wanted to try cycling again. I was not up for a cross-country bike trip. It would be anti-climactic, and where was I going to find 40 days of vacation? We might create some adventure and I was anxious to go. "Look," I said with a thick tongue, "why don't we try something else. Let's try a shorter trip and see how that goes. Then we can build up to something super."

"Great idea," Dr. Hopkins said with enthusiasm. "Where do you want to go?"

"Home…for now. I have to get up at 6 a.m. to get to work by 8:30 a.m., and I'm a little wrecked. What time is it anyway?"

"About 11p.m., but let's spend a few more minutes talking about where we can go."

"Ok, how about north?" We ran various ideas around for a short time, flopped over into a discussion of women, then decided to turn the matter over to a weekend conversation. As we walked to the cars, we both seemed to think a trip down from Canada should be tried in the fall though that did not give me much time to "get in shape." I was quietly concerned as to whether or not I could make such a trip. Here I was bragging about a trip across the country and yet concerned that I would not be able to make it 300 miles down from Canada.

I was bidding Dr. Hopkins goodnight when he asked me to drop the formality and call him Dave, a sure sign of progress. I climbed into the car, plunged the key into the ignition, roared out of the parking lot and arrived at my totally dark little house in 20 minutes.

Dave and I spent more and more time together before our planned trip in mid-October. We were both divorced and weekend dinners usually turned into double dates. Our girlfriends did not want to talk about our plans, which was a fair request and school was kept strictly out of our conversation. The advantage was it prevented us from overkill and allowed us to get acquainted in other areas of our lives besides bikes. Somehow, there was an unspoken agreement that school life and trip planning were separate. For me it was natural as I had always had older friends and in more than one case my boss had become my best friend. There was no problem in keeping these phases of my life separate, and it eased Dave's concern about mixing with students.

Our proposed trip to Canada began to take shape in late September. As we pored over the maps for a likely starting spot, it soon became clear that going too far into Canada would simply take too much time on the return. We were planning a four-day trip, leaving work early on Wednesday evening, boarding a train, which seemed the only logical way to get north with bikes, sleeping the best we could on board and arriving Thursday morning ready to pedal home. After more discussion and a review of train schedules and mileages, we settled on the sleepy town of Saint Albans, just at the edge of the Canadian border in Vermont.

The first thing I had to do was dig out my old bike. Believe it or not, I still had the same bike I had ridden across the country and I never rode again after arriving in Washington, D.C. The bike was in the exact condition I left it with an added coat of dust. A few hours of cleaning brought her to fighting trim. The only thing left to put into "fighting trim" was me. Dave proposed we ride from his house at New Hope, Pennsylvania to the Delaware Water Gap in New Jersey in the last week of September. It would be a distance of 90 miles round-trip. That would be a good test. Could I manage 45 miles in one day? In my mind, it seemed a snap. After all, I had cranked out 145 miles on that last day riding across the country. But how many years ago was that? Too many. So, I decided that the "test" would at least get me better prepared for the bigger trip only a few weeks away.

On that designated Saturday I was fading fast by 2 p.m. We were within six miles of our goal and my legs were in such pain I could barely turn the pedals. The morning had gone fairly well as we roared up Route 32 along the Delaware River. But after lunch, we turned inland at Easton, Pennsylvania and what little strength I had left was immediately sapped at the first hill.

After much carrying on from me, we arrived about 3:30 p.m. A nice little camp was set up overlooking the river, and then we cleaned up, rode a mile to a restaurant, had a nice dinner, came back and talked until I dropped off to sleep. We returned home the next day with few problems. Dave did not bat an eye the whole trip. He had been cycling constantly for years and this trip was nothing for him. My legs wouldn't speak to me for two days but I was sure once they settled down the Saint Albans' run was doable.

Nothing more was done to prepare for the trip. I was caught up in work, Dave was involved with school and weekends were devoted to house projects and dating. I decided to use my ex-wife's newer bike for the trip instead of mine, I had discovered mine had a smaller frame which may have contributed to some of my leg pain. I learned a long time ago that when one rides, the seat should be high enough so that your leg is straight when the pedal is down. Her bike was bigger, newer and, I hoped, in better condition.

With bikes cleaned and ready, a couple of makeshift packs and $150, we met at the Trenton, New Jersey train station at 5:30 p.m. on October 12. We bought two one-way tickets, grabbed a few bottles of coke at the little cafe and walked ourselves and bikes onto the platform where the train was due any minute. As it slowed to a stop, Dave noticed a gorgeous blonde head in the third car. A slight gasp escaped his lips. Grabbing my arm, he turned to me. "Did you see that? This may not be such a bad trip after all!"

The mid-fall sky was already drawing its evening black cover over the sky as the train hissed and squealed to a stop. I was assuring Dave that I had seen that lovely head and that it was not a complete fantasy on his part, as the blue-uniformed conductor raised the steel plate covering the stairs to the vestibule. With the wave of anxious commuters getting on the train, we waited before wrestling our bikes up the three steps. We engineered our bikes into standing positions on the far side of the vestibule, lashing them securely together to various pipes. Scooping up our gear, we ventured into the coach only to find that all this "let others on first" philosophy meant we would be standing all the way to New York. We pressed on through several more cars until spotting what seemed to be the only two remaining seats. With a thankful heart, a slug on the shoulder and a heave-ho with our gear to the overhead rack, we sat down in a heap.

By the time we reached Princeton Junction, we had settled into our long journey. The gear was well stowed and we were already poring over maps. I knew every inch of the road for our proposed trip, but now that we were underway, reading the maps again became more interesting. Maps and general B.S. filled the time as we passed up through New Brunswick, Newark and finally on into the tunnel ending at Pennsylvania Station in New York City. In the hour and 10 minutes the trip took, there was no sight of our little pin-up girl and when the train started up again, after taking on the New York passengers, I proposed a little reconnoitering.

"Yeah, and what are you going to do if you find her?" Dave said with a slight challenge in his voice.

"Bring her back here, of course. Where are you going to sit?" I turned and left with a laugh, neither serious nor sure of what I would do if I found her. As I began slowly walking back through the cars, wondering what overpowering approach I might use to lure this lovely lady to our seat, AMTRAK delivered the suggestion. "Ladies and Gentlemen, the bar car will be closing in ten minutes. I repeat, the bar car will be closing in ten minutes. We apologize for the inconvenience. Thank you."

Inconvenience? What inconvenience? This announcement provided the excuse I was looking for to meet a new friend. As I entered one of the last cars on the train, I saw her sitting alone two seats from the front, her legs casually crossed and fortunately, staring out the window as opposed to reading a book.

"Excuse me," I said, leaning closer so as to be heard over the clatter of wheels.

"The bar car is closing in about five minutes. Can I buy you a drink?"

"Pardon me?" she said looking up in some surprise. My insides turned to a pool of soupy Jell-O. I was awful at this game and was foursquare against rejection. Trying to pretend she simply had not heard me, I tried again and to my surprise, she smiled and confidently said, "Sure."

I was somewhat amazed at my own conquest but not half as amazed as Dave when I walked past him with my AMTRAK playmate of the month in tow. As luck would have it, the bar had already closed so I offered her a cup of coffee instead. We sat down, careful not to spill the slashing coffee, and were about ready to start a *meaningful* conversation when Dave appeared.

"Hi, mind if I join you?" Dave said with a winning smile. I introduced him and in so doing, we both learned that our partner's name was P.J. Greathouse. Within minutes, I was sorry I had made the introduction. Once Dave announced that he was a professor of business, with tonal changes that suggested that the future of U.S. capitalism depended on him, the two of them launched into an esoteric discussion of statistics that left me out completely. It was, of course, understandable that Dave did not see the benefit in changing the subject to some more pedestrian topic within my reach and, in time, I excused myself, comforted only by the fact that it was I who got the ball rolling.

After ole P.J. got off somewhere near Hartford, Dave returned to his seat and little more was said of the event. The evening passed into early morning, forcing us to try to manage some sleep as the train made it's express run up through Vermont toward the Canadian border. It was just breaking dawn when the steel monster shuddered to a stop at Saint Albans, five miles short of Canada. We were among only a handful of passengers that disembarked and with our bikes on the platform began our first real adventure in cross-country cycling.

It was a telling start. I quickly discovered that the air in my front tire was low requiring a stop at the top of the street. The Exxon station was not open at 6:30 a.m., but the pump was outside and working. I cranked the little handle around until the meter indicated 80 pounds of pressure, gently mated the nozzle with the valve stem and patiently held the two together. What I did was promptly blow the tire right off the rim.

Dave ended up on the ground, doubled over with laughter because of the look on my face. Eventually, I saw the humor in all this and agreed that the Bob and Dave Show had gotten off to a good start. The laughter died out a bit when we discovered that the only store in town selling bike tires was closed until 10a.m. on *Thursday!*

I am not sure whether the wave that passed over me was one of anger or depression. We were both a little grouchy from an all night train trip and felt the pressure to get a move on if we were going to make New Jersey by Sunday evening. After stomping around the closed bike shop door for ten more minutes and scratching our heads trying to think of alternatives, there was only one conclusion left.

"How does a two-hour breakfast sound?" Dave finally asked.

"Terrific," I said.

. We were on the main street in town and the restaurant was something more like a truck stop, which meant the coffee was good as least. There we sat for the next two hours drinking coffee, joking and filling the wasted time until the bike shop store owner opened the door at 10 a.m. we were coupled to his backside as he walked in. I got the tire I needed and with Dave's help, made the change in record time. In no more that fifteen minutes we were on the road and ready to start our trip.

The New England countryside during the fall is, of course, legendary. The beautiful leaves paint a plethora of fiery color over the rolling hills creating one of the most inspiring driving experiences America has to offer. Riding a bike through this washboard countryside is a different story. True, the colors were as beautiful as ever, but the ups and downs of the twisty roads were a workshop in pain to an out-of-shape cyclist. I became increasingly focused on my leg discomfort rather than the picturesque countryside. But pain was not the only problem. In fact, it was becoming a minor part of the deteriorating scene.

"Did you special order this rain?" I said, wheezing as the result of my efforts to catch up with Dave who was nearly half a mile ahead. "And did you take the grease out of my hubs? I feel like I'm pushing around lead with this lousy bike." It was too early in the ride to pull over for a break, but Dave caught my drift and suggested a brief stop. His orange poncho was dripping wet from the now steady rain and the cold of these northern parts began to catch up with us.

"Look, I know this is not your idea of fun, but let's not stand here too long. I'm getting cold and we have a hell of a long way to go. I'll slow down a bit and let's see how that goes." We stood around for a few more minutes, then mounted up and began our long trek again.

Ole Healthy Hopkins was far ahead again within half an hour. The rain spat at me as I rode on through the Vermont countryside. By the time I saw him again, it was time for lunch. He had selected a small cafe in some no-name town. The twenty-five mile ride had proved more than painful. Every muscle in my body spoke out a clear protest. Granted, there were not that many muscles addressing the issue, but those present made themselves known. I rolled to a stop next to Dave's bike, dismounted with relief and staggered into the cafe. I quickly found a seat and gulped down a waiting glass of water.

Dave said with a smile, "That was fun. A small bowl of gruel to start the day, defective tires, rain, and hills. Now I ask you, is there any other sport you can think of that you can pay so much to be so miserable?"

"Off-hand, not that I know of. But give me some time, I'm sure I'll think of one. How far do you want to push today?"

"Well, if we're going to make it to New Jersey by Sunday, we have to make 80 miles a day. We've gone, let me see, about 25 or so. That leaves us..."

"Yeah, yeah, I know. Well, let's take half an hour for this and get a move on."

Hamburgers and Cokes were bolted down in record time before we returned to the drizzle and rode on. I was not as uncomfortable as before, but had I developed a new problem. The bike I was riding had a very stiff gearshift lever. I had never ridden this bike prior to the trip and what a mistake. Now I was paying for it. There is a lesson here; don't start a big adventure with untested equipment. I was just sure I could commit this simple axiom to memory. The lever, located on the neck of the handle bar began cutting into the palm of my hand. By late afternoon, my hand was so mangled that I had to tie a shirt around the lever. I simply *had* to be able to move that lever if I was to continue the ride. Obviously, I was trying to avoid any unnecessary shifting, which did little to improve the ride, and I was forced to continue in this condition until we decided to call it a day.

We made camp outside of a small town at about 6 p.m. There was no real rush to set things up. We would have plenty of time for that before it got dark and we could sleep. The truth is I couldn't rush to do anything, I was completely drained. Dave set up most of the camp, candidly. Starting with the orange tube-tent, he found the flattest spot around, drove in the tent stakes with a rock, set it up in no time and shoved in most of our gear. With the bikes significantly lighter, we rode a short distance to a restaurant for dinner, and there, dined on steak and beer. By 8 p.m. we were back at our tent. With little light and little else to do, we turned in early. I was aching from stem to stern, and we were both slightly uncomfortable due to the constant rain. It must have been no later than 10p.m. when it dawned on me that our tube-tent had a small river flowing through it.

"You awake?" I said, punching Dave in the side.

He rolled over, sat up and blinked. "Yeah, I had to get up to rub my side. What did ya punch me for?"

"Have you noticed that we have a small 'water feature' flowing through our little house?" I said, getting out of my soaked sleeping bag. "Do you want to bail or should I?"

"Christ!" Dave said as he bolted out of his bag. We climbed out of the worthless tent into the rain. Slopping around in the mud, we untied the ropes lashing it down to the tent pegs and attempted to reposition the opening away from the oncoming water. Our first attempt at this little maintenance adventure succeeded for a time but not long after we climbed back into our bags, the wind shifted and we were almost back where we started. The rest of the night was spent alternately dozing and fixing our tent. There was little sleep to be had and a fair summation of our life was that it sucked!

The chilly autumn morning brought little relief to our damp spirits. I felt like a dump truck had hit us in the night and, then, figuring that it had, the driver backed up to run over us again. This was supposed to be fun?. I wrung out my bag, which must have weighed 30 pounds soaking wet, and tied it to the bike. While Dave was doing the same, I turned my back and used a nearby bush for the early morning latrine which did improve my spirits somewhat. But it lasted only until I mounted up. There is always a flash of fire that lights up one's groin when you first hit the seat after a day's ride. Dave mounted up with a similar expression of pain and together we painfully rode up the road about three miles.

It was early in the morning but we were able to find an open Laundromat in the first town we hit.. We rode up to the front of the facility, leaned the bikes against the wall and untied our gear.

"How many quarters do you have?" Dave asked as he rummaged around in his pockets.

"A couple. Take these and I'll get some change," I said, handing him fifty cents in quarters. We threw our sleeping bags in the dryer first and laid the rest of our clothes out on the nearby counter. As Dave worked on laying things out I headed off in search of change.

I returned within five minutes and we fired up a couple more dryers. We stripped down to our shorts, placing what we had on our backs into the dryers as well. At 7 a.m. you can get away with that sort of thing. Only we miserable adventurers were there.

The sleeping bags were clearly going to take a while so we put two more quarters in the machine and headed off to the restaurant next door for breakfast (after donning our shirts, pants and shoes, of course). Half an hour later, we returned with bellies full of pancakes and rescued our toasty warm bags.

"You know," I began slowly, "This may have been a fools exercise."

Dave pondered that as he loaded his gear. "I know. The minute we walk out that door, we'll be soaked again."

"Yep," I said with resignation. But we were out here for the sport of it all and this was part of the sport. Some sport. I was beginning to think that riding bikes through the rain, sleeping in wet bags and hurting like I did was not exactly my type of sport.

We stalled as long as we could until finally it was time to go. We rode in silence for more than an hour, predictably soaked within sight of the Laundromat. After a while, it just did not matter anymore. The gearshift wound in my hand reopened quickly.

By about 10a.m., Dave decided, we would not make Connecticut, let alone New Jersey, at the pace we were going. He pulled over to the side of the road and waited for me to catch up. I was embarrassed that I was holding him back but I just could not push that damn bike any faster. Forget the weather, the gear shift lever, and the hills. I had ridden long enough to know that there was something wrong with the bike. It felt sluggish.

"Here, why don't we trade bikes for a while? Let me see how tough you've got it."

"I hate to do this to you, but if you can move this any faster, I will get back on and try harder."

We rested briefly and then made the switch. Within minutes Dave was complaining bitterly about the lousy piece of junk I had given him. On the other hand, the bike that Dave gave me felt wonderful. Rather than leave him in the dust, I fell in close behind and listened to him cursing every time he tried to shift the resistant lever.

We had ridden about ten miles in this much improved arrangement, at least from my perspective, when I could see a railroad track glistening in the rain not far ahead. The track cut across the road at a 45-degree angle so I backed off from Dave's left rear, just a bit, to give him the necessary room to maneuver. As I pulled out slightly to his left, wanting to cross the rails at a better angle, Dave's front tire hit the first rail. Before I could blink, the bike went out from under him. I saw his head bounce off the pavement and I jammed my bike into a wild turn, away from the tangled mess in front of me. I regained control and quickly turned around. I came up to him shouting as I laid the bike down on the side of the road.

"Dave! Dave! Are you hurt?" I feared the worst. If his head had bounced off the pavement, he would never answer me again. But as I ran over to him, I found him struggling to get the bike off his body. His left leg was being pinched by the pedal and his left arm was twisted up under his head.

"Christ, you're hurt!" I said again as I got to his side. I picked the bike up and set it down on the edge of the highway. Then I went back and ever so carefully helped him to his feet.

"Tell me what hurts?" I said, acting as a crutch as he limped to the side of the road.

"Everything, but I can be more specific in a minute," he said with a look of controlled pain all over his face.

Within a few more minutes Dave was much closer to being his old self. What happened was obvious. His front tire slipped on the wet rail and he went down so fast he never knew what hit him. Apparently, as he went down his left arm had flung out, acting as a cushion, preventing his head from actually hitting the pavement. The rest was just skinned legs, cut forehead and minor scrapes.

"Boy, you were lucky!" I said with relief.

"You call this luck?" Dave managed to joke, knowing that it could have been much worse.

I gave him his bike back and we rode on to the next town not more than three miles away. It was near lunch time by then, so we stopped at a nicely decorated bar, Western style, for beer and food.

As we slurped down our first drink, I said, "Uh, I hate to bring this up now, but between my bike, your body and the weather, I don't think we're going to make it."

Dave thought for a bit before responding. "I just hate to quit anything. But I'm afraid you're right."

There was a very long silence but the stage had been set for ending the trip. Now all we had to do was figure out how to manage our bruised egos and a way home. Over the rest of our drinks and hamburgers, we came to accept our failure with more humor and placed a few phone calls to find out train schedules.

"Hey, there's a train leaving in half an hour about two more miles down the road. The next one is at 6 p.m., so let's get our ass in gear and not miss it!" I said as I hung up the phone.

We scrambled to pay the bill, leave a tip, get out of the restaurant and onto the bikes. It's marvelous how energetic one can feel when a goal is in sight, one that's more reasonable. Another lesson; set *reasonable* goals. We flew the two miles to the station near the back part of town. It was not long before the blue engine of the New Haven train could be seen coming down the track pulling only 3 cars We took the last one where we had a spectacular view of the autumn countryside.

After reviewing our trip, we concluded that the bad outweighed the good, by far, including spending a fair amount of cash that neither of us had in abundance. Nevertheless, we explored possibilities for another trip. After all, from the warmth and comfort of our train seats, it had been a grand ole' time! While the train rambled along, we came up with the perfect solution to carrying on our now firmly established tradition of high adventure. "Look," I explained. "I love the sea. If I'm going to pour time and money into something in the future, I would like to try and make it around the ocean. Now you, on the other hand, love cycling. After this adventure, I'm not sure that I want to try and push across the country. It may not be as bad as this, but I remember only too well, thanks to this trip, the struggle it was. So how about this: we could mount bikes on some sort of raft, connect the pedals to a paddle and use our leg power to move a craft through the water, perhaps in the Caribbean. What do you think?"

Dave did not pause. "Are you crazy?!" he said in total disbelief.

"Yes." I said with perfect confidence.

By the time we had reached New York City, I had sold the idea of a pontoon raft powered by pedals. We were pumping out little sketches of the vehicle that would make maritime history. We even had the various routes reviewed, the time involved, and the money necessary. By Trenton, our new adventure was born. Never say die to a couple of diehards. We were going to turn failure into a new challenge.

PADDLEWHEELS TO SAILS

A mutual best friend, Peter Raymond, was reaching for the phone to dial the state mental hospital by the time we finished explaining our paddle wheel-powered ocean-going craft, complete with a model Dave had built from two paper towel tubes, egg carton cups and Popsicle sticks!.

"You guys are very sick," he finally concluded. But, typical of Peter, he did not stop there. He was the Material Manager for Chem-Pump, a manufacturer of very specialized, sophisticated pumps and had access to technology that Dave and I thought we might need but knew nothing about.

"Well, look," he said, "Why don't I take your model here down to the shop and turn the engineers loose on it for a few days? Let's see what they say." We smiled and left expecting nothing.

Peter called back the following weekend, "You won't believe this. I've had three nuclear power engineers working for two days on this crazy plan and they have come up with all the facts and figures."

Late one evening, at his West Trenton home, Peter presented a huge drawing of the proposed craft; we were ecstatic. It was quite a plan. For so many people (that had little knowledge of the sea) to work on an ocean-going vessel was a questionable use of time and talent. But the plan had imagination and we bought into the proposal.

Our pontoon boat was 19-feet long. There were two seats, midship, behind twin bicycle pedals attached to long bike chains running outside the seats and attached to a gear on the right and left side of the paddle wheel. Two-foot high lockers surrounded the front and sides to give us some protection against the sea. The lockers could be removed in seconds, in case of emergency, and were designed to float. What possible emergency would require this safety feature was dismissed as overly cautious. Still, the whole contraption was truly an inspirited creation.

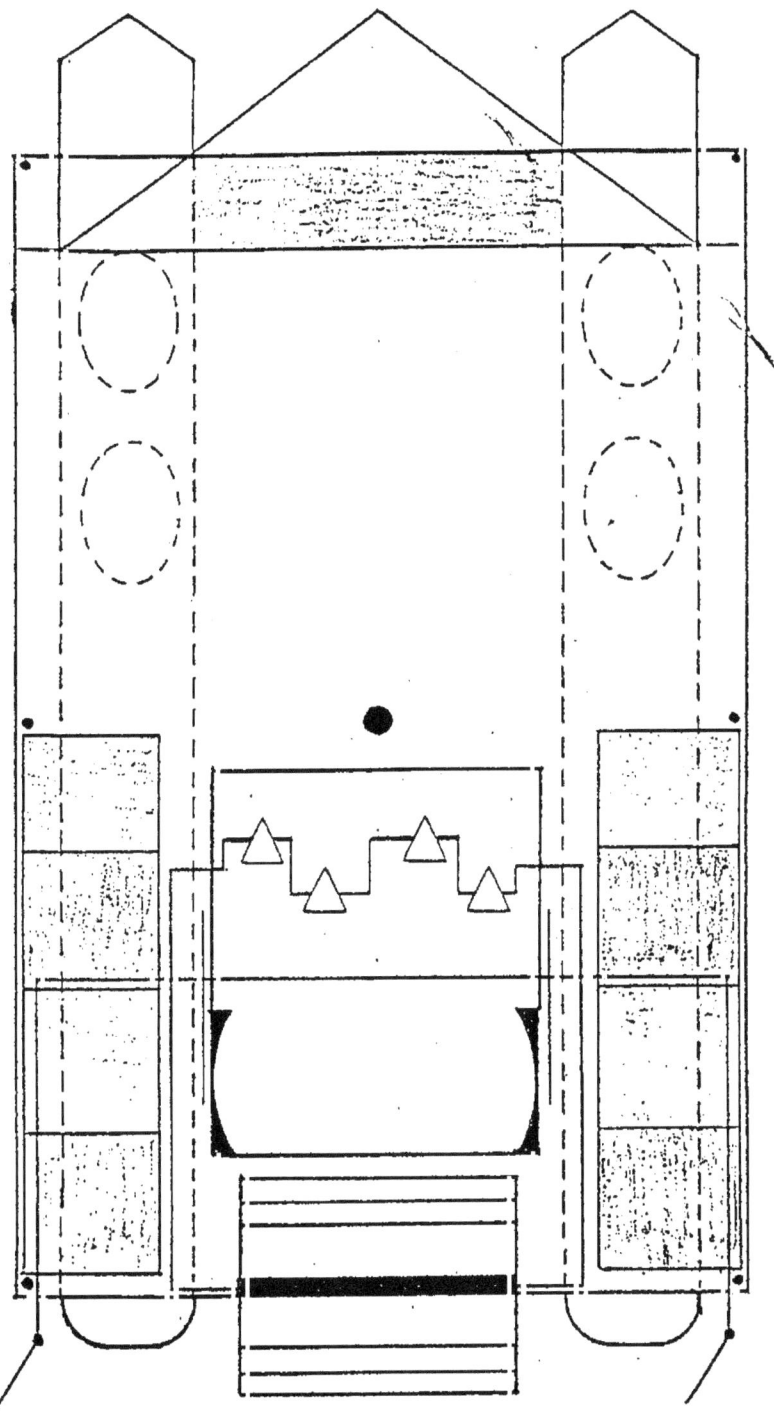

The pontoon bodies were to be made of aluminum and each pontoon was to be three feet in diameter.

Inspired as it might be, it had to be the most bizarre paddle boat ever designed. And what got even more bizarre was our planned route. Dave had concluded the best route was to leave from Port au Prince, South America and paddle our way up the Windward Island chain to the U.S. Virgin Islands to Puerto Rico and on into Miami, in two months! A hero's welcome was expected.

It may seem intuitively obvious to the most casual observer that this plan was 'nuts' from the start, but two reasonably well-educated adventurers were blinded by the possibilities of a *unique* journey. In late March, to promote the "intuitively obvious", one modification was suggested that changed our whole approach. Over beers at the Rider Pub, Dave and I revealed our top secret project to good ole' Ed Higgins. We brought him under control in fifteen minutes and gave him a napkin to dry the tears produced by his prolonged laughter.

"Look, you dorks—maybe you can do all this, but why not put at least a sail on this thing so you can rest?"

"A sail? I don't know how to sail," I said sheepishly.

"Bob, you don't know how to do any of this. What's the difference with a sail?"

"Well. I, er. . . .uh..."

"And besides," Ed went on, "how much is all this going to cost?"

Dave calmly responded with an offhand figure of $12,000 for the whole project.

"Well, why don't you buy a boat for that price; save yourselves all this work and a great deal of embarrassment?"

We finished our pitcher of beer, thanked Ed for his thoughts and walked to the parking lot.

"Shit, I guess it's back to the drawing board," I said. Dave was more reluctant to give up the idea.

Our favorite place for serious discussions was a chic little restaurant in New Hope called "Mother's." Over countless brunches on Sunday mornings we reviewed our progress and reworked our plans but had to relocate, on one fine spring morning in May, after having a particularly bad encounter with the waitress. I was very down at that time - work, projects and women all going badly. I had been very quiet that morning and barely acknowledged the waitress' presence. Finally, at the end of the meal, she came over to the table and announced that I had been the rudest customer she had ever waited on and requested that we never return. I looked up in disbelief but Dave blew up. A fight ensued with Dave defending my right to be a sullen, non-communicative, depressive mental case to the hilt. And after a caustic encounter with the manager, we left steaming. We were out of there for good. Our new meeting ground was my house, where, sheltered from outside hassles, the trip began to reshape itself into a more realistic plan.

I left for three weeks in California at the end of May, and Dave went to Colorado in late June. July was a wash-out with commitments on both sides so it was not until early August that we began to research the possibility of buying a vessel - a 34-foot sailboat. The main problem was simple. We did not have any money. The boats advertised in the newspapers were between $12 -$65,000. I had read that if one is planning to buy a boat, one should purchase the largest boat possible because one will soon outgrow it. That suggested to us that we needed something in the thirty foot range.

Due to finances we seemed doomed to something in the 18'-22' range. Without knowing much (read: anything) about sailing, that size boat seemed too small for island hopping in the Caribbean. It was August 12, 1977, a Saturday morning, when Dave called to say he had found a 25-foot boat for $5,300.

"Great! How big is the hole?" I asked. "I'll be over in 30 minutes; let's call and find out."

I made the journey from my place to his in record time, and we called the seller the minute he arrived. From the description over the phone, there didn't seem to be anything wrong with the boat. Could we come over? No, they were busy, but the boat was down at the Atlantic Highlands Marina. We could see it and if interested, could call to set up a mutually convenient visit. We raced for the car and off to the Highlands we went, stopping briefly at the top of the street for Wawa coffee to go. We found the boat which looked OK but was not rigged. She was yellow, there was no hole and came with a travel trailer—that was about all we could determine. With nothing more to go on, we left and spent the day roaming boatyards up and down the coast. Everything we saw was $12-$20k and none could be hauled around on a simple trailer. That evening we called about the little yellow boat at the Atlantic Highlands Marina. The crazies wanted to buy it.

On a Tuesday evening Dave and I rallied at my house near 7 p.m., and with growing excitement we drove off for our second nautical encounter. The boat had been moved to the couple's small backyard near Atlantic Highlands. This gave us a chance to climb on board and inspect everything. While surprised to find the cabin an empty shell, I was quietly pleased to find an implied woodworking project. I loved woodworking and within five minutes I had built a splendid interior cabin in my mind. Dave was skeptical.

Our mixed reaction to the boat was not the case with the sellers. The couple that met us at the small Atlantic Highlands Marina looked like hippies from the Sixties. However, through extended conversation, he turned out to be a Ph.D. computer analyst working at Bell Labs. She had a Masters in Engineering. Impressive.

Why did they want to sell their boat? As it turned out, they had just bought a 35-footer and planned to sail along the coast of North America for a year. My kind of people! I don't know where the words came from, because we had no money, but I said, "We'll give you $4,800." Dave looked at me as if I had just sold his sister. Jim and Pam, our seller/host, looked at each other and silently communicated. After thirty seconds of apparently highly sophisticated eye contact, Jim said, "Agreed."

A few Heinekens were lifted to our deal and out we marched. We drove home delirious. We promised to figure out where the money was coming from in the morning. Somehow a policy had been implemented which was to be with us until the end: Shoot for Mars, and if that's impossible, do the reasonable and fly to the moon.

Our spacecraft – <u>The VENTURE 2-24</u>

"This graceful craft offers more living room, ease of handling, safety and high performance than any competitive boat. In our opinion it's the largest sailboat that can be easily trailered with a retractable keel. Is easily ramp launched and safely trailered. It is the fastest of the Ventures, and has built up an enviable racing record……."

…..and the "You had us at hello!" description:

"For sheer pleasure, try spending a weekend on anchor in a secluded cove…away from everything but the sun, the breeze and the blue sea. Try driving the board hard in an exciting race or a fast passage to a new harbor. Every day will be different, and every voyage will be an adventure."

Half-off Sail

VENTURE 2-24

This graceful craft offers more livable room, convenience, safety and high performance than any competitive boat. It is one of the larger sailboats that can be safely ramp launched and safely trailered. The 2-24 is one of the fastest boats of its type and has built up an enviable racing record.

LEARNING TO SAIL

The monies necessary were assembled surprisingly fast. We needed $2,400 each, cheap for a 25-foot sailboat. Dave acquired the money by applying for a bank loan. Since he was in debt up to his thinning hair, there had to be some sort of credit check involved. But it was approved and he had his share. I did the only thing my budget could stand. I sold my life insurance policy which brought in $2,535. It might be observed that the one thing someone wants when learning to sail is life insurance, but this was no time for pessimism and it was a legitimate source of funding as opposed to more nefarious means.

With cash in hand, we went over to see our new boat. Pam and Jim had everything ready, and the plan for the day was for them to take us out and show us the "ropes." It was a pleasant Saturday in mid-August, but the wind was light so no great speed records were set. In fact, there was hardly any movement at all. We were making two or three knots at best. But speed was our last interest. We needed to know the basics, like how to rig the fool thing. Jim made it seem simple enough but at the time, it was hard to know what we really knew. The only thing to do was to take it out sailing on our own.

It was at that point, we ran into the first of several hundred problems. After working out the money, making countless checklists to determine what we had with our new purchase, and what we needed to make our new purchase actually work, we forgot one major item.

"Dave," I calmly said on our way home. "How are *'we'* going to tow *'our'* new boat around? You have a Dodge Colt and I have a VW bug."

"Oh, Christ! How did we forget that one?!"

"Well, let's spend a few minutes delegating blame" I said. "Do you want to take it or should I?"

"You take it!"

"I was hoping you would. Perhaps I should rephrase the question. How come your Wharton School of Business-like mind forgot that we needed a car!?"

"Let's look at this from a different angle. Whose idea was it to buy a boat in the first place?"

"Ed's."

"Good—let's blame him."

"Agreed!" And, fortunately, we could laugh at our stupidity.

Jim was good to us. He hitched his 1957 Ford Econoline Van up to the boat and towed it to my backyard the next week. With the huge yellow purchase in my rather small backyard, we were ready to begin the enormous task of learning to sail. For openers, Dave had to be on the road the last two weeks in August. I was unable or unwilling to wait for him to make the first trial sail and went in search of a car and crew. The only answer that came up was to enlist my girlfriend. Her father had a Lincoln Continental and she had two younger brothers, Tony and David. What could be more perfect? A crew and car all ready to make my first sail easy as could be. I rented a trailer hitch and on the first Sunday in August, this collectively unschooled nautical team set out for the big event.

I drove this untested combination to Perth Amboy, the waterfront town on one of New Jersey's busiest shipping channels. Eventually, I found a launch site but one with a very steep gravel ramp. The first attempt to launch was a predictable disaster. Fortunately, my skill at backing up a 25-foot boat trailer was pretty good—although I cannot imagine where I learned this practical art. From wherever it came, it served me well the rest of the day. Threading the boat down this narrow ramp was quite a trick, especially on the casually aforementioned loose gravel which turned to mud when the trailer dropped off the edge of the ramp. By the time the back wheels of the Lincoln were in the water, the boat was still a foot *out* of the water. High tide may have done the trick—but this was not the spot.

Exactly how I got the boat and trailer out of the soft mud with the back tires of the Continental kicking up all kinds of loose gravel remains a mystery. Fearing the worst, I started up the ramp and to my amazement, the car moved forward and the boat followed. I brought it out on to the street, everyone quickly piled back in and we were off in search of a new ramp.

Carteret was the next town up, where we found a fairly good public ramp and dock. It looked more promising so once in position at the top of the ramp I raised the mast, rigged the boat, set up the engine, and put on the rudder before backing her down to the water's edge. An hour later, after several attempts to get the boat off the trailer, we were tied up to the nearby dock. The motor was eventually started, the dock lines were retrieved and off we went. The 7.5 hp. Sears Gamefisher engine quit not more than a few minutes after we started. That was great comfort for an inexperienced captain and crew! We were out for a sail so rather than try and restart the engine I decided it was time to set the sails.

The wind was very light, which was good for a first sail. I knew enough to have one of the boys bring the boat into the wind whereupon I spent the next thirty minutes trying to figure out

Half-off Sail

which line went with which sail. I finally did get it all hooked up right and raised both the main sail and the large front sail called the genoa. In the light wind, nothing spectacular took place, thank God. I turned the tiller over to anyone who'd take it. No one did, so assignments were made: Tony (the older) was ordered to the tiller, David posted as watch to look ahead, and Donna sunbathed. I worked on the temperamental engine. After 40 minutes of having my tail high in the air and chest hung over the stern to work on the engine, I was interrupted by a casual call from David.

"Uh, Bob. You better look at this." I looked up. The boat was headed straight into a rock pile not more than ten feet ahead on the Staten Island side of the Bay. The rocks were supporting a light buoy and they were stacked almost like a pyramid. The rudder was all the way to port, but the light wind prevented any course change. My hand raced to the starter cord. Two pulls told me it was not going to start. I grabbed the tiller, from Tony and, more out of desperation than knowledge, threw it all the way over to starboard. The bow swung completely around just missing the rocks. As the stern followed, it lightly bumped the stack of rocks just below the water line.

"David, watch the bow!" We were pulling away from the rocks but heading straight for a small fishing boat directly down wind and in our path. The fisherman leaped to his feet and helped fend off our slow moving sailboat with quick hands and a few under the breath curses. I brought the bow further around so the wind was abeam to gain speed.

Things settled down a bit, but I was left to wonder why David had waited until ten feet in front of the rocks to alert me. Rather than say anything negative, I mentioned something about "it could happen to anyone." After all, who was I to talk? I hadn't a clue what I was doing. But the thought of punching a hole in our new boat before Dave even got aboard added greatly to my massive anxiety present from the time we left the backyard.

We headed out to the channel center but within 15 minutes, I felt the centerboard bouncing on the bottom. We were 200 feet from the shore, and I couldn't figure out why we should be hitting ground.

"Tony, pull up that goddamn centerboard!!" I needed action and Tony just stood there.

"How?" he finally said.

I had forgotten he would, of course, not know what a centerboard was. I raced forward and furiously cranked it up. I later learned that those little bobbing metal objects in the water were there for a purpose. They were channel markers and I was way off course. Shorelines mean nothing. Charts and buoys are your guide. There was so much to learn.

My outburst had brought a protective sister into action. Donna blasted me for talking to her favorite brother in such a fashion. I needed that rebuke like a hole in the head but, rather that have a mutiny on my first command, I suggested we head for home.

After ten minutes, the engine started, the sails brought down and I motored up the Arthur Kill River against the strong outgoing tide.

The closest I could bring the boat to the dock was ten feet. The current was too strong, and my skill at controlling the boat at low speed was poor. Also, I was fearful of shutting the engine down knowing how tough it was to start. Someone needed to get the car and back the trailer down to the water so I could run the boat straight onto its' skids. Since we were all on the boat and the *Force* was definitely not with me, prayer, magic or sacrifice was required. Fortunately, David volunteered to jump in and swim ashore. He did, but he had no idea how to back the trailer down into the water. After a good half-hour, he finally managed to line up the car, trailer and ramp so that I had a reasonable shot at ramming the boat onto the trailer. Donna spent the time profitably; she harassed me about my unreasonable demands on her brothers.

I powered the boat onto the trailer I was relieved to have the boat and all of us on dry land. It was only after I pulled the trailer and boat out of the water that I noticed it was totally off-center. With Tony guiding me from behind boat, I began backing the trailer back down to the water. It seemed tough, as if the wheel was blocked by something. What should have been handled by just braking actually required a slight touch of the accelerator. Something was not right, but I could not figure out what. Tony finally came around to the driver side window and said that I had better stop. I got out, went to the back of the boat and my heart skipped a beat. The rudder rope had not been secured. The rudder is divided into two sections. When each half is in line, or straight down, the rudder is set for sailing. It is hinged in the center so the lower half of the rudder can be brought up to 90 degree angle so it is out of the way and clear for travel. The rope holds the rudder in either the down or 90 degree up position. I had put it up to move the boat on to the trailer. Somehow, it had slipped and dropped the lower half of the rudder down causing it to drag on the ground. With Tony watching, I had backed right over it, cracking the upper unit in two. I took the whole thing off, backed the trailer into the water, repositioned the boat so it was centered, pulled the boat/trailer to a flat spot at the top of the ramp and secured everything for the trip home. The trip home was made in complete silence.

It had been quite a day. The boat had nearly been holed on the rocks, I ran aground. I broke the rudder, and I was about ready to break up with my girlfriend. So this was yachting?

Yet, I couldn't wait for the next trip, but before I set foot on the boat again, I thought I should consult a psychiatrist. Dave returned the next week and turned ashen when I told him the story. We reviewed it again and again to learn more, but it shook us both.

"Before we sink the boat, shouldn't we have a name for it?" Dave said after exhausting the stories of its' first voyage.

"How does *Reef Finder* sound? Perhaps, *Sir Leak Allof?*"

"Or how about *Tangle Foot?*"

I was sort of thinking of something that summed it all up. Does *Porco di Mare* strike a familiar chord?"

We were having fun with this, but I had the name I really wanted. While on Crete, on vacation, many years ago, I read a book on mythology. I swore to myself that "if and when" I ever got a boat, I would name it Nereus. Nereus, I had read, was the father of Poseidon. It meant kind and gentle winds and best of all, he had fathered fifty sea nymphs. My kind of god!

And, after further discussion, my lobbying effort succeeded. Our new boat, for as long as we should have her, was to be the Nereus. Her? Nereus is a guy. But, for whatever historic maritime reason, all boats are 'her' even with a masculine name.

The next trip made the first one look easy. A windy Saturday in early September found us heading back to the public launch at Perth Amboy, New Jersey. Only this time, the Nereus did not wait until it was in the water before it started protesting a return to the sea with such an unskilled crew. It tried to leap off the trailer en route. I can't say that I blamed her. If she had any sense of what was to come, her maneuver was more than justified. I stopped the borrowed truck and inspected the problem. Sure enough, another Fuller foul-up. In my rush to get home from the last sailing disaster, I had forgotten to lower the centerboard into the "V" on the trailer. That little neglected point would have prevented the boat from walking off its cradle and, more importantly, taken the weight of the 300-pound centerboard off the boat while bounding along the numerous New Jersey Turnpike pot holes.

The trip proceeded slowly with prayer. Although we had used a whole roll of duct tape to tie the boat to the frame of the trailer and continued on our way at 20 miles per hour, we were convinced there was mutiny still in the making. Worse still, going 20 miles per hour with a boat half on, half off the trailer, up the New Jersey Turnpike, was sure to attract the State troopers—a humorless lot. This was less than desirable because our trailer lights weren't working (why would you expect them to work?) and rumor had it they tend to make you leave the trailer where it is until those little problems are fixed.

The prayers must have worked. It is the only logical reason we made it to the launch ramp. Before we tackled the job of setting up the mast and rigging, we just sat in the truck, sipping coffee and nervously munching on bagels and cream cheese. I had rebuilt the upper part of the rudder after the last trip, so it was ready to go;

and the engine had been gone over thoroughly. But we seemed in no rush to get underway. An hour later, all was ready and the boat was magically in the water tied up to a nearby pier and ready to go. The engine coughed to life within thirty pulls on the starter cord and we motored out in the Raritan Channel with the idea of setting the sails once out in open water. The day was rather windy and it seemed like a good idea to give ourselves plenty of sea room.

Raritan Bay was once a sought-after resort area. The now-sleepy town of Perth Amboy still hosted waterfront mansions and the Perth Amboy Yacht Club, a fairly prestigious hangout for boaters. But the channel leading north from the Amboy's, toward New York City, is trafficked by very large commercial vessels. It is no place for small sail boats. The tide was ebbing. We weren't familiar with the power of tides, but we did know that we were riding this one out. We rocketed under the Outer Bridge Crossing and into the widening channel which joined the Raritan River to form the bay.

The water quickly got choppy in the brisk wind. It was a chilly day with a light haze. At the obviously appropriate spot, just past the sign that says *Raise Sails Here* and with Dave at the tiller, I began working on raising the mainsail. We were making mistakes left, right and center at this point. What *should* have been happening was that the bow is brought into the wind and held there while the sail was run up the mast, free from any tension. During my hourly commutes by bus to New York City every morning, I had read every book on sailing I owned and they all tell you "bring the bow into the wind." Did we do that? Not a chance. Instead, our first coordinated effort to raise the sail turned into a rout.

Dave put the engine into neutral, at my brilliant suggestion, which cut our speed to a drift. With the boat jumping from one direction to another I struggled and struggled to raise the sail. Without forward movement, the rudder was almost useless. The boat would drift to one side, and the sail would catch the wind, forcing me to fight every inch of upward movement. Buried in a wildly flapping sail, I called for Dave to come back into the wind, where upon I would be fighting to prevent the sail from diving into the water. Dave was watching this scene with equal tension but managed to laugh for both of us.

Finally, the mainsail was set, but what happened next gave us both a chill. The boat was unstable and directionless with just the mainsail up, and she heeled way over. Actually, not knowing how much of a heel the boat could take before turning turtle caused great alarm. The slightest heel seemed too much. But this was more than slight. We went wa-a-a-y over. The thought of raising another sail seemed as if it would only add to our troubles. For all our lack of experience, more sail seemed counter-indicated, yet we had to balance the boat.

I decided to take out the jib, the smaller of our triangular shaped sail for the front. On a radically pitching deck, I try to hook the snappy clippy things on the sail to the forestay, the wire rigging that runs from the near top of the mast to the tip of the bow. The jib is supposed to be clipped to that forestay and hoisted to its full height by pulling on the halyard, a rope attached to the top of the sail that goes up to a pulley on the mast and then down to the deck where I could reach it. It took twenty minutes. The whole time I was hanging on for dear life with the sail repeatedly smacking me in the face and the deck dancing under my feet. With tremendous effort, I attached the jib and raised it into position. Once set, the boat did seem more balanced. We were now out in the center of the bay. The shore no longer offered protection, and the full force of the gusting wind played havoc with our attempts to keep the boat on a reasonable course. We hadn't yet learned to let the sails out for a course across the wind. This lack of understanding caused us to heel far too much.

"Dave!" I called over the roar of the wind. "Let's take her back. This is too much!"

"Right!" Dave swung the tiller, and rather than make a clean tack, we were instantly locked in irons, meaning the boat would not steer either way. Whatever we were doing we were doing it wrong and prevented the boat from coming about.

"Try it again," I called. "Get some speed up and then hit it hard. I'll walk the jib around!"

Again, we tried with no luck. Finally we jibbed, that is to bring the stern rather than the bow around into the wind, just to get headed back up the channel. A gust caught us again (the sails were close-hauled when they should have been loose) and we went way over again.

"One more of those and I say we take those damn sails down!" I screamed, hanging on to the life line.

"Hell, yes!" Dave called back almost ashen. And sure enough, it happened again.

"Lower those sails! I'm going to start the engine." Dave scrambled forward and had the mainsail down in seconds. The engine started with two pulls and I grabbed the tiller, brought the boat back on course and began stuffing the mainsail into the cabin. Just as Dave lowered the jib and the boat leveled off, I heard a sickening "whap" and the engine immediately died.

With sails down and no power, we were in a hell of a mess. I quickly looked over the transom, and to my disbelief, saw a green plastic trash bag wrapped around the propeller, trailing behind.

"You're not going to believe this," I hollered. "We've picked up a passenger."

Dave didn't believe it. Again, I hung over the transom and began pulling away the entwined plastic.

"I'm going over. I can't get it from here." I said, taking off my parka.

"It's freezing in that water, you can't go in!"

"Just steer," I said as I jumped in. I wished that I had listened to him.. It *was* freezing. I worked furiously for about a minute and made little progress. Dave grabbed me as I tried to pull myself back into the boat. Thank God he did. My arms felt like lead. I stood there with my soaking wool turtleneck dripping red dye all over the cockpit.

"We've got to do something fast. We must be making 4 knots back out to sea!" Dave exclaimed.

"Aim for the shore. I'm going to pull the engine into the boat and work from here."

I quickly released the fuel line, untied the mounting bolts and dragged the motor over the transom.

"How are we doing?" I said, out of breath.

"You have about four minutes until we hit. I'll bring up the centerboard"

I grabbed a pair of pliers, unbent the cotter pin, spun the nut free, pulled off the prop, pulled free the entwined green plastic trash bag, slammed the prop back on the shaft, tightened the nut, replaced the cotter pin, swung the engine back over and began reattaching it.

"One minute!" Dave called.

I pumped up the fuel line now reattached, set the choke, pulled the starter cord with vigor, released it, pulled again....and we hit the Staten Island shore line.

"Well, at least we're safe—for the moment," Dave said with some relief.

I looked around. On either side of the boat, old pilings stuck out of the water. How Dave managed to miss all those obstacles left me completely baffled. He had apparently hit the one stretch of open beach.

I was exhausted, very cold and needed to get out of my wet clothes. As I dried off it was agreed that we would take a lunch break. Fortunately, I had a partial change of clothes. The meager lunch supplies were set on the table and with growing relief, we made ourselves bologna sandwiches.

"We're do'in pretty good," Dave finally said with a laugh.

"Yeah. We're alive and still have a boat," I mumbled with a mouth full of dry meat. "You know what strikes me about all this is we're not learning from all those books were reading."

"Well, I haven't read all the ones you have," Dave challenged.

"Right. And I should know more than I do. For example, we should have let those sails out more. I just wasn't thinking. And why did we run aground? We could have thrown the anchor out."

"True. But have we ever used an anchor?"

"No."

"So we didn't know what to do. I don't even know how deep the channel is. The chart says 35-feet, which it may be. I don't even know if we have the necessary sixty feet of chain to set the bloody anchor in that deep of water."

"True... well," I said after a moment's thought. "We have a lot to learn. By the way, why is the boat rocking so much?"

Dave thought a moment, and then leaped up. "Christ! The tide is going out!"

We raced on deck. The water was lower. We jumped over the side, hit the beach with a thud and with all our might tried pushing the boat off the sandy beach. With the centerboard up, Nereus only drew 18-inches. But once the tide dropped, we were hopelessly aground. We both went nuts.

Being aground is not that big a deal. One simply waits for the tide to rise and you're off. But, in our case, it seemed like a disaster. The first thing we did was find objects we could stuff under the hull to prevent the boat from rolling into the narrowly missed pilings. Fortunately, the beach was littered with spare tires, and we gathered about six to form a cradle under the keel. Then, there was nothing to do but wait. And wait we did—for seven hours.

Since there was nothing else to do, we decided to tour the town. Actually, there was no town, but a scattering of gas stations, liquor stores and other small enterprises. I called Donna to tell her I doubted I would make our Saturday night date.

"You what? If this boat is more important than me, we're going to have trouble!" Donna said with the fury of a stood-up, red-headed Italian.

"No, no. You see, we ran aground and I'll be back as soon as possible."

"Why did you run on to the ground? Don't you know how to steer?"

"Well, yes... no... you see it was because we..."

"I don't want to hear all these excuses. I'm going shopping!"

"Well, maybe you could drive out and see us. We're only 15 minutes from your house."

"No. I have to go shopping."

"Ok. Talk to you!" I slammed down the phone. I almost screamed at Dave, "God damn-it! Here we are in a mess and she's pissed at *me*!"

"Right. Let's get a six pack."

I steamed around for the next hour while Dave chuckled as we slowly finished several cans of beer. The alcohol had a quieting effect and since I was now in no hurry to get back, the wait seemed more tolerable.

We returned to the boat by 3:30 p.m., and sat in the cabin finishing our beer. Finally, toward dusk, we began preparations for departure. Dave cleaned up the cabin and I worked on the engine. We had to make sure everything worked properly when it was time to push off or we would be in real trouble.

At about 4 p.m., we could see a man climbing down the small bluff overlooking the bay. He was carrying a small pot of coffee and other goodies we could not see. As he approached, he waved a greeting.

"Saw you fella's come ashore earlier. Thought you might like some cheese sandwiches and coffee. Gettin' pretty chilly out here."

We were overwhelmed by his generosity. My girlfriend couldn't drive 15 minutes to help, but here a stranger came out with snacks.

"Say," he finally said. "Why'd you fella's motor ashore so fast? Lots of pilings out here. You're lucky you missed 'em."

I had a mouth full of cheese so I let Dave elaborate. "We didn't motor ashore. Our propeller got caught in a plastic trash bag and the current swept us ashore."

"Oh,... you guys were lucky." he finally said, rubbing his chin.

"Well, best be gett'n back. Tide'll come for you about eight."

"Not until then?!" I was aghast.

"Yep. Good luck to ya."

We could not get over the generosity of this stranger. Then, about 5:30 p.m., our work was interrupted by a lone stroller coming down the beach. He was long-haired, supported a scruffy beard on a youngish handsome face, dressed in dark blue trousers and a dark blue work shirt, reasonable attire for a walk down the beach except that he had no shoes or jacket. As a result, his feet were sickly blue as well as his hands. It was cold and for some reason this wanderer chose this time of year to dress like spring. As soon as he spoke, I knew why.

"Hey, man, life is groovy! Peace be with you."

"Oh, brother," I said under my breath and continued to work.

"He-e-ey; how're you fine people this fine day? Mind if I have some of your food?"

"Dave," I whispered urgently. "This guy's a schizophrenic."

"Are you sure?"

I had worked for years in a nearby mental health center and knew only too well. "Yes, I'm sure." My normally tolerant self was in no mood to take the special time this guy would need. For the next hour and a half our space cadet circled the boat talking to himself. We busied ourselves with little odds and ends for something to do until our pending departure.

By 7:00 p.m. the darkness had started to blanket the bay. Little lights appeared along the opposite shore and from where we were it looked quite pretty.

Then our crazy buddy began, "Why couldn't they just leave all the land the way it was? Why did they have to fuck it up with all those buildings and factories?"

"So people can live, I suspect," Dave chided, tongue in cheek. I'm sorry he said that because our friend's brain was somewhere near outer Pluto, and that was all he needed to hear.

For the next half hour he rattled on, to no one in particular, about how beautiful life could be without all those man-made structures. I studiously avoided any conversation. Dave tried a few lines, but got back such gibberish, he wisely gave up. Finally, the loon asked for a ride across the bay. I exploded. "Look, buddy. I can't get this boat to where it needs to go let alone an excursion of the harbor. Absolutely not, and would you kindly let us be!"

I came wading back out of the water where I had been cleaning trash bags from the incoming tide with my boat hook. The poor fellow took one look at the pole and said, "If you want to hit me with that, well, it's ok." "I don't want to....ok, never mind." I walked to the other side of the boat wanting desperately to concentrate on getting the Nereus ready, not run an outdoor psychiatric clinic.

By 7:30 p.m. the water had reached the boat. A little longer and we could push off. I stood at the stern, ready to clear away other floating garbage. When the water was almost high enough for refloating, I started the engine. She came to life after a couple of pulls. After Dave gathered up the anchor buried on the beach, he was ready to put his shoulder into the bow. At 7:50 p.m., we were pushing hard and the boat broke free from the beach. I jumped on board and Dave walked her back, guiding her as far as he could. Just as he turned the bow up-river, our emotional handicapped traveler came wading out with his pack over his head.

"Dave, get on quick!" I had the engine in gear and was slowly running ahead before he was completely aboard. But, even with that, our would-be hitch-hiker was working hard to catch up. I could not imagine throwing him off, but that was what I was prepared to do. I worked away from the shore as quickly as possible, applying increased power as evenly as the engine would take. Finally, we were far enough out. I watched the desperate man turn back to the shore. He could use the bridge close by, but in a strange way, I suspected he never really wanted to go to the other side. He wanted friends, and I, for one, failed him miserably on that score. Thank God!

I worked us out to the middle of the channel. We were in a bit of a fix. There was no radio or any other means of communication and the boat was only partially refitted so we didn't have running lights rigged. We had not expected to be out at night and had only one hand-held flashlight to let other seafarers know we were out here in the dark.

I was seated and held the tiller tightly with my right hand, my left ready to adjust the engine at the slightest hiccup.

Dave was standing on the bow with the one flashlight signaling directions. And then it happened. The one thing we could least afford. The engine coughed, sneezed and sputtered to a stop. I swore, grabbed the starter cord and gave it a pull. It almost caught. I pulled it through with vigor and found myself flying back into the cockpit. I looked up at the starter cord dangling in my hand. I had pulled the cord completely out!

"Christ, Dave, we're really in trouble!" I screamed. "I broke the engine!"

"Oh, shit! Well, you'd better hurry and fix it because we're coming up to the bridge pilings."

"I can't fix it. The start cord pulled right out of the engine!"

"It did what?! Oh, double shit!"

I fumbled around in the stern locker and found a paddle. "Here, take this and fend us off those pilings, if necessary."

Dave ran back and grabbed the paddle. As he took it forward, I maneuvered us to the middle of the channel by swinging the tiller back and forth trying to use the rudder like a paddle. If the current didn't play tricks on us, we could shoot between the bridge towers without a problem. The current was strong and took us up-river at a good clip and thank God it was going the right way. I was staring ahead like a hawk, all my senses on high alert. Dave began paddling to give us a little speed for better maneuverability. He paddled until his arm was about ready to fall off so I went forward to paddle until my arm actually fell off and was eaten by lobsters. Then Dave came back to the bow, took the paddle and I went to the tiller.

We had been at this for a while when I looked back and noticed some lights very high over the water. At first, I thought I was looking at a floating factory. The lights and darkness play funny tricks on the water. When I looked again I gasped. It was not a floating factory at all. It was a supertanker coming up-river with a tug on each side! "Dave, up the power!" I called with as much control as possible. Dave gave me a funny look but began paddling harder. The tanker was gaining.

"Dave, seriously up the power! We're being followed by a supertanker!"

"WHAT!!?"

"Just keep up the pace!" I jockeyed our powerless, lifeless boat around to the near side of the channel. The tanker was still coming. It was about a hundred feet away and looking like the USS Missouri from our little yellow raft, when all of a sudden the whole harbor lit up. The tugs had finally spotted us. Horns went off, loud speakers blared and the starboard tug went racing around to the tanker's stern. I held my breath. Dave was paddling furiously now and I was moving the tiller back and forth to add speed. The truth, I was working furiously with no effect. The tanker appeared to stop in mid-channel and slowly come completely sideways. My heart was hammering louder than the pulse of their engines.

I really don't know what happened to the tanker. We sped along, pulled by the black conveyor of incoming tide water, and the whole flotilla disappeared from view as we rounded the bend. Within another several minutes, our little dock was in view and, again, swinging the tiller from side to side, I worked us closer to the shore. If we missed that dock, we would not have a second chance. It came closer, Dave readied the bow line and threw it just as I brought the Nereus almost straight in. The line caught something, Dave fended off the bow, the stern swung around, and we were safely where we wanted to be, gently bumping the most positive stationary object we found all day. For a long while, we just sat neither counting our blessing nor cursing our day, just numb from the hairline down.

By the time we pulled ourselves together and hauled the boat out of the cold water, it was about 9:30 p.m. Without trailer lights, we towed Nereus home completing my second, and Dave's first, sea trial. Some sport. Few would argue that we had had some trial! Most would wonder how these adventures could possibly encourage further use of this or any other boat.

PRACTICE RUNS AND CONSTRUCTION

Before I went out sailing again, I had to make two phone calls. One was to my best friend, a psychologist, who had known me since graduate school days at Princeton Theological Seminary. I needed to find out from Dr. Powell if my behavior could be looked up in a textbook. If yes, my "never-say-quit" push to learn sailing could be reduced to sheer pathology, and I had better stop before I killed myself. The other call was to my parents. After a vague conversation, they assured me my IQ was greater than 20. I ducked their question as to why I wanted to know, and I hung up comforted by the fact that I was just uneducated, not dumb. Dr. Powell filled in the rest by pronouncing my condition as "idealized stubbornness."

Armed with these positive checkpoints, I was prepared to try again. I don't know what got Dave back out on the boat. Our first trip had been his first ever on the water, and where he found the strength to go back after all that, I can't imagine. But, return we did. It was the next weekend, as a matter of fact. He brought Shelley, his girlfriend, and I brought my latest purchase. There was a car dealer at the top of my street. By chance, I had seen a 1977 Ford Ranchero in the window. It was discounted as a close-out, so I sold my 1967 VW for $1,000, took out a loan for the remainder and bought the car. It was perfect for our needs. The only drawback was the color: brown with flaming orange pinstripes down the side—a real California car if ever I'd seen one, and looking quite out of place in New Jersey. But, with a comfortable interior, reasonably powerful engine and pick-up truck open bed, it made the local trips and proposed big adventure to Florida look more manageable. Step by step we were becoming more committed - if not financially, at least materially to this massive undertaking.

It was growing late in the year for sailing. We were, in fact, one of the last boats on the water for our second run in early October. This time we went to Atlantic Highlands, the exact spot where we bought the boat. The logic was that perhaps the familiar waters would help Nereus feel more at home. We also had a *new* Sears 7½ horsepower Gamefisher air-cooled engine (bought on sale for $265). The other engine was just worthless in my mind. We were beginning to experience the old law of the sea; a boat is a hole in the water into which one pours money. I hadn't expected to buy a new car and a new engine in October. Dave was a teacher so he was broke. The equipment purchases were my burden if this trip was going to happen.

The launch went well and even the motor trip out of the harbor went smoothly with our new engine. Once out into the bay, it was "sailing as usual." I decided that since setting up the mainsail first had caused such imbalance last time, I would set the jib first. I did that, but what happened next left me hopelessly depressed. While trying to set up the mainsail, Dave could not keep the bow into the wind. The boat just leaped around in circles, throwing the jib sail from one side to the other. I finally sat down in utter despair. If we couldn't even get the damn sails up, how were we going to learn the fine art of sailing?

It was discouraging work, capped off by the loss of one sail bag overboard. But we finally did get both sails up and with only shallow enthusiasm, made a short run around the harbor. We pulled Nereus out by early afternoon and drove home in less than good spirits.

Meanwhile, other matters were happening at a ferocious clip. I was enrolled in my last course for my master's degree at Rider

University. Dave was the instructor for my last course and, aside from an occasional problem of maintaining a straight face when some reference was made to 'planning ahead' or 'controlling variables', things were OK. We were able to separate our academic and personal lives nicely. The two never crossed, and I took the course in statistics just like anyone else. That was on Monday nights. On Wednesday nights, Dave met me in New York City where we were enrolled in a Coast Guard course on "Basic Boat Handling." It was fun. Not only did we learn a great deal, we always went out for a beer afterward and reviewed countless details of our proposed voyage. Other nights were devoted to construction. The Nereus had to be rebuilt inside. Fortunately, I was very good at wood working and as fall moved to winter, I turned the house into a small factory. The basement was laid out for cutting and sanding. And I began building the obvious first requirement: a wine rack. The second floor study was turned into a staining, varnishing and drying room. The living room was for study. Countless books on the sea, charts from everywhere in the Caribbean, manuals on everything starting with 'how to open a safety pin', navigation material and the beginnings of our equipment list - all of which was spread out everywhere. But my real love was construction.

Out of a hollow shell, I slowly turned the cabin into two separate rooms divided by a beautifully mahogany stained birch bulkhead, complete with a finely fitted door. One of my first steps was to line the whole hull interior with cork panels. This not only provided decoration, but insulation as well. From the interior walls, I began reconstructing the front cabin or vee berth. Starting with the unusable space at the tip of the bow, an anchor chain locker as well as three compartments were installed, suspended from the deck. This allowed space for a bed. The next fixture was a four-bottle wine rack carved with the letter "N" for Nereus. This was on the starboard side. It was followed by a three-foot long bookshelf under which I mounted a tape deck. Under the vee berth were mounted two batteries where cables ran up to the control panel just behind the twin vee berth bunks. The control panel was a combination storage hold on the bottom, bookshelf in the middle, followed by contoured instrument panels on top supporting a plethora of switches, gauges, radios and RDF. A chart table folded back against the bulkhead, allowing the occupant to either sit and study charts when the table was down, or turn around and use the seat for what it was—a porta-potty. A floor-to-ceiling mirror added a sense of space.

On the port side was a floor-to-ceiling locker divided into compartments for food storage. It was the most complicated cabinet I ever constructed, with so many angles, that to this day I am not sure how it held together. All wood was stained in a rich brown supporting six coats of polyurethane.

On the opposite side of the bulkhead was the main cabin. On either side of the seat attached to the bulkhead were cabinets with interiors resembling something of a jigsaw puzzle. Each cabinet was divided, and each division allowed for one or more specific items to be stowed in a customized cradle. The design supported the landlocked belief that all things could be secured. This, among countless other mistaken beliefs, was to prove wildly optimistic. The table itself was made of inch square birch boards cut to various lengths, creating a beautiful butcher block effect. The galley actually was mobile. When not in use, it slid under the cockpit. This open space allowed for seating or sleeping. When pulled out along the port cabin, it served as a countertop four feet long with panels lifting off for the two-burner stove and sink. Underneath were dishes, cups, silverware, pots, pans and cleansers; each in their specially designed space.

Lockers were numbered so that quick instructions could be called out *in an emergency*. The numbering system proved practical in subsequent journeys, but it was also the brunt of countless jokes. "Was that 4a or 4c where you think the can opener lives?" The floor was carpeted in garish orange; the seat covers were stripped of an ugly yellow vinyl and reupholstered in a soft brown naugahyde, window curtains were patterned, a brass clock and barometer added the final touch.

In a way, this was the real purpose behind the Nereus. Yes, sailing *might* be fun—if we could get it right. But it is the beauty and comfort of the living space, at sea, that makes it all worthwhile. It is, after all, home and should be the very best.

Winter, that year, was not long. Night after night was spent working, reading, studying and talking. I lived alone, dating Donna only on the weekends. She did not share my interest in the sea, and it was fortunate we did not live together. The battle over my preparations from both a time and money perspective would have been non-stop.

By February I had graduated. Dave and I were teaching a course together at this point. Thomas Edison College hired us to teach a course for New Jersey state employees. The students were working toward their BA degree at night. Our course was Communication Skills. Two guys who could not communicate well enough to raise a sail or remember to buy a car were teaching others the art of communication. Scary. But we enjoyed our work together and found team teaching among our strengths. The only flaw in our efforts came when we learned, after about the sixth class, that one of our shyer students—a woman in her mid-forties, was no longer in class because she had been shot by her husband. We theorized that she had gone home, one night, and tried to create an "honest and open" dialogue with her husband who had not had the benefit of our course, and, bang! That ended that conversation. Some teaching we were doing.

The NYC Coast Guard course was over by April. We had both passed the test and received a piece of paper that assured us and others we were now competent seamen. Yet we were anything but confident. As the days grew longer, we were faced with the challenging reality that our trip was fast approaching.

"God knows, we aren't really ready for this," lamented Dave one night. "But there's no other time in our lives that all the pieces will be so perfect. I'm not married....yet. You're not married… yet. Both of us plan to re-marry someday. We don't have kids and we have some time and a little money. Most of all, I can get time off from teaching and your boss will let you take six weeks off. My

God, we aren't ready, but when are we ever going to have such a combination? We have to go."

"Right, I'm not fighting you. I just think like you do. We don't know what the hell we're doing!"

So we both knew the score, and read even more books to try to diminish our fear.

"Dave, what is your worst fear? What is the very worst thing that could happen out there?" I asked one evening after a good dinner, a bottle of wine and some good music.

Dave took a long time to answer. He seemed to be weighing his words carefully. "Well, I'll tell you. I'm a little afraid of the water, for openers."

I sat bolt upright. "What?! You never told me that!"

"Sit down, you turkey. That's not what causes my knees to shake. What scares me most is thinking about the night. Being out at sea at night with waves crashing all around and then from out of nowhere the boat catches a howling, screaming wave sideways and flips. Then I'm out in the cold ocean, you're gone, the boat's gone and I'm alone, fighting against the sea. Then all of a sudden, two big phosphorescent green eyes five feet apart appear on the surface..."

"Holy SHIT! The very thought scares me just sitting here! Ok, ok, I'm sorry I asked! Where'd you get such a nightmare?"

We sat there thinking of the creatures ready to greet our voyage. The rest of the night was a game of; Can-You-Top-This? While our worst fears came out of those evening sessions, a new itinerary did as well. From our brief encounters with the sea, we re-examined our proposed routes with more reality. We decided we would no longer take on the whole Caribbean. Rather, we would be fortunate to manage a voyage around the Bahamas, perhaps even to Exuma, an island just 90 miles off the Florida coast, if we were lucky. That shift was the key. We were now talking about sailing from somewhere in Florida to the nearest island rather than a costly ferry ride to some all-too-distant tropical paradise. We were, as some loudly observed, learning. Above all, we were making the trip more reasonable. Of course, the reasonable thing would be not to do it at all.

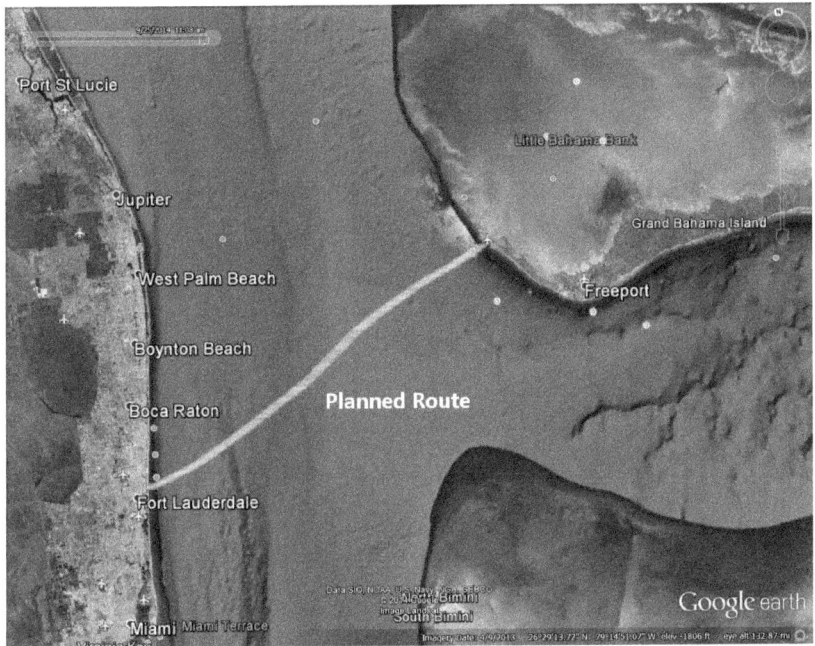

Perhaps we could wait another five years, try it with a bigger boat and more sailing experience. That was clearly the smarter play. But, we didn't think we had five more years and the vision was more compelling than taking all the necessary steps to ensure *living* through the completion of what now was a goal; sail this year, ready or not. Then, in mid-April, another event occurred that created another shift in our thinking.

For a change of pace, Dave, Peter, Mack (a friend of Peter's) and I borrowed two canoes for a day trip down the Delaware River. This was to be no major event, just fun for all; a break. We loaded the two canoes in the back of the Ranchero, plus Peter and Mack. Dave, Shelley and I sat in the warm, comfortable cab as we drove the 125 miles up-river.

By 8:30 a.m. we were on the water and Shelley was on her way home to wait for our "come pick us up," call later that afternoon. The day was pleasant, the sun was out, the water very cold, and partners were switched throughout the day for variety. On the last leg of the journey, nearing New Hope, PA., Dave and I got in the same canoe and took off like a shot. Peter and Mack seemed to be having a time of it trying to coordinate their paddle work, so we throttled back and made pleasant work of our final run. Before the others reached a small dam, about 5 foot high, just past New Hope we decided to use the time to scout out a good portage around the last obstacle on our trip. After all, no one short of an Olympian would go through the spill-way, in the center, or, worse yet, over the whole thing. When we came to the end of the dam, near the New Hope side, discovering it was not good for portage, I just happened to look up and saw Peter and Mack shoot directly *through* the spill-way. Their canoe literally stood on end, in the violent turbulence, rolled over 180 degrees and disappeared. I saw two heads come up with two sets of arms flaying widely trying to survive the broiling river.

We went into a power paddle for the opposite shore that could have set a world's record. We slammed the canoe into the shore and Dave ran some three miles downriver to the point where Peter and Mack finally made it out of the water. I followed, far behind, arriving to find both swimmers safely ashore. The fact that they were alive was almost a miracle. Another couple of minutes in that icy water and something serious would have happened. As it was, a shore-bound fisherman saw all of this, radioed the rescue squad and the ambulance was pulling up to the canoe almost at the same time the guys were coming out of the icy water They were frozen stiff, shaking uncontrollably, and in shock. They were also very lucky! If near death could happen this close to home (Peter's house was no more than five minutes down the road) on a river, what exactly was it we were trying to do by going off to an open ocean in an untested sailboat, with no knowledge of the area and 1,200 miles away?

It was a chilling thought.

PREPARATION

There was a go, no-go discussion about our upcoming trip that came up almost daily. But, in our heart-of-hearts, we knew there was no stopping us. For all our questions and fears, we were set for this adventure. Although not everything was going according to plan, things seemed right on schedule since there was hardly any plan to follow. All we had, really, was an end in mind. We just had no idea exactly how to get there. It was fortunate that this was so. Under the growing pressure, our true personalities became apparent - as personalities always do under pressure. Dave had revealed features closely resembling a borderline obsessive/compulsive personality. That is, he had a strong drive to never accept defeat, to never quit a plan and to fret over every detail. Once something was set in his mind, he made it happen. Fortunately, the one compatriot feature normally associated with this trait, the obligatory drive to always assume command and micro manage everything, he lacked.

I, on the other hand, suffered from more the hysteric-type personality. I was ready to try anything. I had that loose-as-a-goose, southern California style of thinking which frequently carried me into trouble on the more structured East Coast. I paid scant attention to details and one could frequently drive a truck through the loopholes in my logic. I was more the visionary, the grand planner-type. Interestingly, the very demands of our preparation lifted the best features of both. Neither Dave nor I assumed "command." It was one of the most constructive, easy-going, non-competitive relationships I have ever enjoyed. We both tackled jobs for which we were best suited. While I blasted ahead, Dave molded the progress with the necessary focus. But things happened to each of us that we learned only in retrospect. Imperceptibly, the whole project changed some of our basic natures. We adapted. Dave was doing something he would have never tried because he never thought it possible. And I was becoming attentive to detail like never before. The very activity of putting a ship and voyage together demanded enormous planning and attention to detail, which I found quite comfortable. I was beginning to discover that when I was very interested in something, like saving my life, I was *very* detail oriented. Dave's more rigid side yielded to a more fluid approach to planning. He was exploring problems and comfortable with incomplete answers.

Spring brought a rush of activities and changes. If work was intense during the winter, it grew to a fevered pitch by May. Things were changing rapidly on the personal front as well. The conflicting relationship with Donna had forced a temporary break-up. I dated a little more and even tried reconciliation with my soon-to-be ex-wife. That lasted three weeks. The old problems then quickly resurfaced. I began dating a girl in New York whose brother was crew aboard the Petrol, a classic old sailing ship in New York Harbor. I hoped he would invite me aboard and teach me to sail. It never happened. So, between the expense and without obvious prospects, I curtailed that area of my life almost completely.

Mid May also allowed us to once again try our hand at sailing. We made two short day sails with better results, making a total of five trips for me and four for Dave, before heading south for the open sea.

Not a solid preparation to say the least. On the home front there was a staggering schedule afoot. Dave prepared a detailed list of all equipment, necessary food, safety gear and monies required. The list itself was intimidating. Dave had been doing a running check list since the purchase of the boat. The major pieces were in place and most of the carpentry work was done. But it was the list of "little" things that became overwhelming. For example, one small necessary item was a first-aid kit. Well, take a look at what we needed for that alone:

First Aid Kit:
Solarcaine spray, Polycillin, Iodine, Phisoderm (antibacterial), Hydrocortisone, Sodium bicarbonate, Eye drops, Ophthalmic ointment, BFI first aid powder, Milk of magnesia tablets, Decadron tablets, Aromatic ammonia, Darvon, Sea sickness pills, Bacitracin ointment, Aspirin.

First Aid Supplies:
Thermometers, Cotton balls, Eye cup, Scissors, Vaseline, Ace bandages, Gauze bandage and pads, Medical adhesive tape, Band-Aids.

The rest of the list was truly mind-boggling. It included:

Sailing Equipment:
Awning (Cover the cockpit area), Sailing gear and rigging, Winch handle, Halyards, Fittings for halyards, Repair cable and clamps for forestay/backstay, Shackles, Turnbuckles, Cotter Pins (selection of sizes), Sailcloth (to patch tears in the sail), Assorted lines for rigging, Ropes for securing the boat to docks or other boats.

Electrical:
Batteries (flash lights), Assorted Wire, Volt meter, Pliers, Screwdriver set, Wire cutters, Electrical tape, Soldering gun, Solder, Fuses, Lamp bulbs, Running light bulbs.

Spare Parts for Outboard Engine:
Spark plugs, Oil Filter, Spare fuel line, Hose clamps, Engine oil.

General Equipment:
Lights (flash lights/kerosene light), Swim fins, Diving mask, Snorkel, Spear gun, Camera, Film, Shark repellent, Life Jackets (4), Sun hats, change of clothes, swim suites, Tarps, Knives (cooking/utility/fishing), Books (Jaws/ Famous Shipwrecks/The Bermuda Triangle Mysteries), Logs, Pens, Chart (Straits of Florida-#11013), Book: <u>Sailing the Abaco's</u>, Maps (Mid-Atlantic and Florida for drive down), Flares and flare gun, Ladder (getting out of the water into the cockpit), Mirror, Anchors (bow and smaller stern anchor), Flags (Bahamas, US, distress), Spare parts (for mechanical and rigging), Horn (canned air).

General Tools:
Hammer/Mallet, Nails(4pd/6pd), Screws (assorted), Screwdriver set, Saw, Hacksaw, Drill (hand operated), Drill bits, Paint brushes (2), Polyurethane, White paint, Stain, Putty/Putty knife, Sandpaper (assorted grain), Extra Wood for Repairs.

Navigational and Basic Equipment:
Radio, Depth Finder, RDF (Radio Direction Finder), Compass, Hand-held wind speed indicator, Watch, Binocular, Raft, Fishing Equipment (2 poles, tackle, line, etc.), Ice cooler, Motor (9 hp outboard), 12 Volt car battery, Battery terminals, Boat hook, Scissors (large), Bilge pump (hand operated), Stove (two burner Coleman Camp Stove), Fuel (4 Propane bottles).

Miscellaneous:
Clothes detergent, Dish detergent, Kerosene (small amount in a can), Shock cords (Bungees), 4 Fuel cans (gas for the motor), Three magnet catches replacements(for cabinets), Two pails, Watertight box, Sunglasses, 4 jugs of distilled water, Suntan lotion, Insect repellent, Toilet paper, Toilette articles, Clothes pins, Comet, Baking Soda, Soap, Soap Container, Lysol, Toothpaste, Toothbrush, Dental floss, Glasses Strap, Jumper cable, Gloves, Rags, Travelers Checks.

Kitchen:
Utensils (for two), Cutting knives/serving fork/spoon/peeler/can opener), Small kettle, Small Teflon frying pan, Two sauce pans, Four cups, Four plates, One mixing bowl, Cutting board, Small coffee pot, Cork screw.

And last but not least:

Food:
Crisco, Coco Powder, Coffee, Powdered Milk, Tang, Cereal (single serving instant packets–Oatmeal), Pudding, Coffee cake, Canned peaches/pears, Canned vegetables, Canned stew, Lemon juice, Salt and Pepper, Seasonings, Aluminum foil, 4 bottles of wine, 1 bottle of Gin and for the remainder we plan to buy fresh produces on route and spear fish for most of our dinners.

If we had to go out and buy all this, the medical list alone would have been well over $200. Back to Peter we went. Fortunately, his wife, the nurse, had resources. She went through the medical list with us and was able to "borrow" almost everything we required. .

But this was just one small package on the boat. Consider assembling such a list for "spare parts" on electrical gear, fishing, equipment, engine repairs, navigation, emergency equipment, food, etc. Then figure out where to stow it. While my carpentry skills were good, the sheer volume requiring placement in a 25-foot boat lent an air of the impossibility to the whole adventure.

Dave always divided our endless lists into <u>Have</u> and <u>Need</u> columns. It was so rewarding to move a check mark from the need column to the have column that we sometimes just went out and bought items so we could check them off. But the real stumbling blocks were the big items. Things like radios, RDF's (Radio Direction Finder which allow the user to plot the bearing of various radio waves relative to your vessel creating a roughly 5 mile triangle indicating your location. This is all pre-GPS), and batteries were so expensive we were hard pressed to know exactly where the money would come from to make the needed purchases.

As it happened, word had reached my parents about all this and the fact that one major safety item we lacked was a radio. This "leak" was probably similar to ones we receive from the White House. In other words, it was by design on my part. My parents had enough fear for my safety, with good reason. They felt the one thing they could contribute to my well-being was funding for our radio. The $500 was gratefully accepted, and I installed the aerial and radio in the first week of June.

Our planned departure was set for June 12. The pressures to complete all the work mounted. As luck would have it, the plumbing in my house decided it was time to join the act, and on June 2nd, my water stopped flowing. It took me two days just to determine the problem. First, I thought the pump was broken. Peter, now my personal quartermaster, came over to take a look. After testing the suction for a day in every possible way, we could not figure out the source of the problem. The pump worked, but no water was brought up from the well. Then Dick Neff came over. He was an engineer from DeLaval and my neighbor from across the street who had had similar problems with his house. But after both these pump experts looked at my system, *they* were baffled. Finally, I dug up the well. After replacing the check valve and reassembling the whole system, I tried it again. It still didn't work! There was only one pipe left: the three-foot section connecting the well to the house. I pulled it out, after hours of work, and found a one-inch hole causing the problem.. That evening—four days after all this started, I took my first shower. It's great to learn how to plumb your own house and who your friends are, but I lost four solid days of work on the boat. Time was growing short. With an all-out push, aided by Peter and Dave, I put the last coats of polyurethane on my handy work.

We loaded the boat and car Thursday night and Friday morning. I said goodbye to the only living things around me that I still loved, my dog and cat, to be cared for by a neighbor, and we drove off. We made it a tenth of a mile down the road and stopped at the car dealer at the end of my street. Our trailer lights were not working and we begged a friendly mechanic to give us a hand. He fixed it in about an hour. I slipped him $10, and we were now really on our way to somewhere near Fort Lauderdale, Florida.

The two-and a half-day drive was comparatively uneventful. Our only concern was for the trailer tires. With only two tires supporting several thousand pounds of boat, they tended to heat up. We were compelled to pull off the road every two hours and hose them down at any friendly gas station. Once past Washington, D.C., the gas stations became markedly friendlier. Whether or not we really needed to do this would have probably caused a tire salesman to laugh but it made us more comfortable.

Our hours in the car were far from wasted time. In fact, it proved to be an excellent time to review the whole trip. We comprehensively reviewed detailed lists from food to supplies of all types. We tried to account for every spare nut and bolt. Our biggest problem was trying to balance the need for redundancy to manage almost any disaster we could think of to being over supplied. We even divided disaster into levels with detailed procedures to follow. For example, if we were starting to sink, Dave was to work the radio and remove necessary items from the forward compartments. I was to inflate the life boat, secure necessary equipment from the stern locker (let's see, that would be # 6), start shooting the flare gun and try to steer, if it mattered. There was hardly a combination of problems we could imagine that did not have some plan or thought aimed at preparation. Whether it would actually work *under fire* was another question but thinking things through was valuable. Coming up with some of these scenarios, like "the hull cracking in two" or just plain "sinking" seem to add to our apprehension rather than create a sense of comfort due to adequate planning. I found we sometimes just changed the subject rather than finish some of these disaster recovery stories.

We slept in the boat the two nights on the road. The first night we made it all the way to Enfield, North Carolina. It was 10:30 p.m. when we pulled into a liquor store parking lot. We judged the

Half-off Sail

location to be less than ideal especially with an open Ranchero full of supplies. I was on edge the whole night but successfully managed my anxiety with a constructive and comforting approach. I slept with a loaded flare gun. Can you picture me waking in the night, thinking I heard something and firing a flare gun into someone? Dave could because he didn't sleep at all. The night passed uneventfully and we were merrily on the road by 7:00 a.m. Route 95 was flat and boring, except for the South of the Border billboards in North Carolina. It was the kind of road that enabled us to continue talking and concentrate on driving at the same time. The boat seemed to get into the rhythm of the interstate, comfortably following us at our steady 50 miles per hour. Anything faster and she would start fishtailing. Late Thursday afternoon found us in St. Augustine, Florida. We pulled into a campground on the beach not far off the main highway. A swim and campfire made for a pleasant break. By 2:30 p.m. Friday afternoon we were at the public dock in Pompano Beach. This was the launch site recommended by several people who knew the area. We gently set the Nereus in the water, rigged her and while Dave loaded a number of supplies, I asked the police patrol boat if it was OK to leave the car and trailer in the parking lot for a while. I was assured that there was no problem. We left the boat tied up and the trailer in the lot for an hour while we drove over to the Sands Marina to inquire about dock space. There was room, and, for $12 per day we had a shower to boot! Things seemed to be going smoothly. By local ordinance, we could not sleep on the boat overnight unless we were at the marina. Since we surely would not be there more than a day, $12 seemed manageable.

We drove back and parked the trailer in some out-of-the-way spot at the public dock, boarded Nereus and motored out into the main channel for the trip down to the marina.

"Dave, how the hell do we get under that?" I gasped in astonishment as we approached our first drawbridge.

"I don't know. Let's watch the other boats do it."

I circled the Nereus in front of the bridge several times until another sailboat came up. I heard three blasts on his whistle and shortly afterward, the bridge came up.

"You don't think...." I started to say.

Dave cut me off. "Let's read the Coast Guard manual about drawbridges when we tie up."

I carefully watched the mast on the first boat as it passing under the draw bridge. It seemed tricky, but since we did not plan to do the drawbridge number very often, I resolved not to get too involved with learning the fine art of navigating between bridge uprights and we slipped right through.

By 5:00 p.m. we were tied up in slip 23 and headed for the showers. One thing was immediately clear about Florida; the slightest exertion caused profuse sweating. We were soaked just setting up the boat and could not wait to shower. By 6:00 p.m. we were having our first cocktail on the boat. For the first time, it felt like we were living the dream!

The next morning we walked the two miles back to the car and drove off to the local A & P where we spent $230 on six weeks of food supplies. At the boat supply dealer, another $103 was spent on odds and ends; a Bahamas flag, charts, voltmeter, spear gun, a box of fuses and the like, which were all loaded into a couple of cartons and carried back to the boat.

The remainder of the day was spent in the exhausting work of stowing all our supplies including crawling under the cockpit to position supplies in containers that could be easily pulled out when needed. We must have reloaded everything ten times to get the combination right. Water bags were filled to capacity, gas cans loaded, the mast light repaired—everything in readiness for departure the next evening. Our last night ashore justified a fancy steak dinner. Once back on the boat, we were all set for departure.

What we actually got *set* for was to wait. Florida had never seen such bad weather. Storms at sea, thick grey/black clouds and sometimes sheets of rain brought us to near depression for the next four days. There was nothing we could do but wait.

We passed the time talking to a crazy yachtsman named Pax who claimed to be an ex-CIA agent and JAL captain. God knows if any of his stories were true, but they made for good listening. By Wednesday night we were so depressed we called Peter. After a 15-minute chat, we walked down the road toward Hillsboro Inlet, our departure spot and watched the boat traffic until a little after 8:00 p.m., then hitched a ride back to the boat. The boat was where we wanted to go but our completely stoned driver took us some five miles down the road to a local disco where we were assured of a good time. By 11:00 p.m. we were bored and broke. Five miles home seemed like a long walk so I stuck out my thumb. Within two minutes, a police car pulled up.

"You boys really don't want to be hitchhiking."

"Sure we do. It's five miles back to our boat."

"Yeah, and a night in jail if I catch you hitchhiking again!"

"Right, Officer. We don't want to be hitchhiking." And so, we walked and walked and walked. At midnight, Dave broke into a rousing song of Happy Birthday. It was June 20th, my birthday. Some birthday. I was 31, we still had some two miles to walk and we were still on dry land. By 1:00 a.m. we were back on board in the lowest of moods.

The next morning, the weather broke…slightly, but by early afternoon, it was fair. We resolved to begin our trip rather than pay any more money for the slip. The bill was paid, we dropped the lines, and by 4:00 p.m., we were motoring toward Hillsboro Inlet. We were on our way! We later found out that Peter had flown down that day and came to the marina only an hour after we left. He was doubtlessly going to provide motivational therapy. It was only the beginning of several near misses.

NIGHT OF TERROR

All too quickly the night closed in around us. Black clouds, in the west, shuttered the twilight and extinguished the twinkling lights that were visible from Pompano Beach only minutes before. Once out of the Inlet we had managed to set both the mainsail and jenny with relative easy. To the casual observer, we *might* have looked quite professional. Whether or not anyone else was on the water had escaped my interest until now. All at once, we were very alone on a dark and snarling sea. Our world was reduced from wide majestic vistas to our immediate surrounding and we were plunging ahead into an unwanted isolation. If the Walt Disney Imagineer's needed ideas for a future version of Mr. Toad's Wild-Ride, they could have joined us and gained all the scary ideas they could ever use and still have people pay for the experience. I was just beginning to understand the insanity of yachting. We had paid dearly to be out here.

The boat lurched forward as the wind picked up. The only sure sign of progress against the ever changing three-foot watery crests and valleys was a trail of white foam curling behind our stern as we clipped along at an impressive six knots. The trail was erased with each passing wave and I became glued to the compass, our infallible direction finder in the consuming void. "Always believe in your compass," I could hear my old flight instructor saying. "When everything else gets confused, your compass does not." I repeated the reassuring words over and over as the night unwrapped more confusion and chaos.

Three hours had elapsed since we had left the safety of Hillsboro Inlet. This was our first venture into a real ocean; forget the relative peace and security of Raritan Bay, it was our first attempt to sail at night, which quickly made day sailing seem like a walk-in-the-park. It was our first *storm* at sea. That was too many first's for comfort. We were decidedly on edge and feeling even more disoriented with each passing minute. The ocean, the night and the storm were enough to turn two card-carrying chickens into florid aquaphobics. Couple this with the feeling of being lost, and all the elements were present to turn our fit little boat into a floating rubber room.

"Think I'll go below and get a 'fix' on our position before things get worse," Dave said with a concerned look to the northeast.

"Great! You think things are gonna get worse?!"

Neither of us had our sea legs and any movement was difficult. Our little ship, the one we had once put on par with the U.S.S. Nimitz, was responding more like a little yellow cork bobbing haplessly on a washboard ocean. Dave crashed from one side of the companionway to the other, knocked his head on the hatch cover, stumbled through the opening and was seated twice before he reached the galley table.

I could hear him saying to himself, "Christ! I can't even fight my way inside, let alone find out where we are!" Then, in his best Inspector Clouseau voice, he looked up at me and said, "And, if you will try and miss these bumps, I will get to work."

"Try and miss the bumps. Right?!" I said to no one in particular and kept my focus on the job at hand. I could not even see the bumps, let alone miss them. It was not more than a minute later when I heard Dave banging around under the cockpit not far forward from where I was standing. What was he doing under there? Things weren't bad enough yet to merit seeking refuge under the cockpit, though, the more I thought about it of it, maybe they were. The wind was now at twenty knots and seemed to be strengthening. The sea was piling up four and five feet and whoever was directing this show gave the unmistakable impression that things *would* get worse. Before my refined skill for pessimism was working fully, Dave's activities below became clear.

Boxes were being moved from one side of the cabin to the other. The search continued until I heard Dave exclaim, "I've got it!" Another minute passed and out through the companionway came a safety orange rain slicker and Dave. "Here, put this on. You're going to need it anytime now."

"Terrific! Where's yours?"

"Oh, well, I'll be down here working on the RDF, so I won't need one. Besides, I think we only have one set of foul weather gear. You know, we really should pack this stuff in a more accessible place."

Dave disappeared below before I could question him as to why we had not packed multiple suites of foul weather gear when we planned this cruise to the sunny Caribbean. I was left alone with my thoughts and the humorless position of being the one to stand out in the wet and cold. This humorless circumstance turned downright nasty when it began to rain two minutes later. Trying to put on foul weather gear in the rain while steering a wildly pitching boat almost outmatched my skills. By the time I was finally suited, Nereus was considerably off course. My complete attention was devoted to correcting that problem for the next half hour. It seemed like everything conspired against holding us on the 80 degree heading that had been so easily established on the chart. Waves and wind sent the Nereus on a wild, drunken course from wave top to wave top. One piece of good fortune did offset the otherwise frightening panorama before me. The wind was coming from the northeast at just the right angle to allow me to keep the sails close haul (close to the centerline of the boat) and take the waves at a forty-five degree angle. While there was obviously too much canvas up, the course was almost textbook perfect. Nereus would climb up sharply to meet the top of an oncoming wave, then rocket down and across the back of the retreating wall of water. This tactic held us reasonably close to our course and was far better than taking the waves head on. Dave was still getting tossed around hard however. . If he was to find our location, I had to somehow flatten the ride. I could see he was spending most of his time grabbing one loose item after another.

"Bob, you've got to hold her steady. I can't lock in on the radio beckons at this rate!"

"I've got my hands full up here!" I hollered back. "But, let me try something!"

With body taut, I swung the tiller to port and brought the bow parallel to the waves. If I could get the whole boat rising and falling with each passing wave, it would stop the sharp crashing. This armchair theory of storm management might have worked if I had not forgotten one thing—I did not let the sails out.

Whack. The lee rail went into the water. Dave flew across the cabin again, and literally bounced off the wall. Gear not already under Dave's protective care found new unlikely homes. I was busy grabbing for the lifeline trying to stop my sure departure from the radically pitched deck. We were still heeling sharply when I grabbed the main sheet and released the pressure on the main sail. Having too much canvas up in these winds was stupid and problematic enough, keeping the sails close hauled was suicidal. With the pressure off, the boat slowly righted herself and I plunged the tiller back to starboard in an effort to bring the bow back into the wind.

"What the hell are you doing up there?!" Dave screamed.

"Just trying to make you more comfortable!" I screamed back. What I was actually thinking was that I didn't know what the hell I was doing.

"Well, you're doing a hell of a job. Try the less comfortable route. I'd like to live!"

"We just have to get some of these sails down! Get up here as soon as you can!"

Dave waved his acknowledgement. Before he could return to his work on the RDF he had to relocate most of the equipment he was using. Dividers, rulers, flashlights, charts and the radio itself had flown all over the cabin. A food locker dumped a special offering of cans of Campbell soup, mixed vegetables, beef stew and steamed corn all over the floor. Dave worked on cleaning up for a good ten minutes before setting up shop again.

But, at the time, I was too busy to see all this. The wind had picked up sharply around 8:30 p.m. and made steering an Olympic event. The driving wind created driving rain. Night blindness and the near horizontal rain pelting my face brought visibility down to zero. It's hard to judge the true speed of the wind in a storm at sea, at least it is for a neophyte sailor. The noise is disorienting. One minute the boat is on top of a wave and completely exposed. The sails whip and snap frantically along their trailing edges. The rigging sings and whines under the strain. And salt water peels off the tops of the waves, arriving ahead of schedule with a sting to your face. Worse, there is the brackish taste that will leave the heartiest sailor begging for a piece of Trident to prevent mouth corrosion. In the next second, the boat is screaming down the backside of the wave and into a trough. The noise softens in this almost protected channel and the sails go limp. There is a split second of rest before the world turns back into primeval chaos. If modern man is ever interested in getting in touch with his Cro-Magnon roots, then a storm at sea is the best vehicle. Nothing is stable. Nothing is level. Nothing is familiar. There is no horizon and there is no sky. It is an all-black, one-dimensional universe whose action cannot be stopped.

I judged the wind to be racing through the rigging at about thirty-five knots. Had the wind been coming from any other direction, we would be requiring rescue rather than endurance. The forty-five degree angle off each wave was our best strategy. We were sailing close enough into the wind that should anything more serious happen, I could come up two degrees and stall the boat by pointing directly into the wind. However, the wind direction also created one major problem: huge waves.

The waves were now reaching heights of ten and twelve feet. It was the result of the wind blowing directly into the oncoming Gulf Stream. The Gulf Stream is a river in the ocean flowing across the deep waters of the Atlantic until it reaches the Caribbean Island chain where it hits a natural dam. The result is that as the Stream swings up through the chain and northward along the coast of Florida - it flows rapidly and in some spots the flow is up to six and seven knots. In the Straits along Florida itself, some twenty miles off shore, it flows about four and a half knots due north. It was the area we were now sailing. The two opposing forces, the wind blowing in one direction and the water moving in the other, made waves more mountainous than usual. What might have been high rolling swells, had the wind combined with the water to move in the same direction, now were high, sharp peaks of foam and waves. It made the ride more like a rodeo event.

I struggled with each passing wave to get back in line for the next challenger. Even the slightest error in hitting the wave at forty-five degrees made a loud clap as the wave came up and literally smacked the upturned bow with tons of sea water. I imagined a large neon sign announcing another victory for the ocean in the Nature versus Visitors duel. Nature-5, Visitors-1.

My hands were full trying to thread our bow through this narrow corridor of seaworthiness, Dave's position below was worse. I was on deck, in the wind, fresh air and rain totally absorbed in my work. Dave was inside, trying to read small numbers on poorly lit pages and follow a bouncing needle on a constantly moving radio.

"Dave! Are you alright down there?"

His voice was almost a whisper. "I've barely got one line on the chart and that's the one out of Hillsboro. Can't raise any other signals in this weather…. I'm sick…..can't you keep this thing on course?"

Dave was never going to work the Radio Direction Finder in this weather, so we could not know where we were. We were under heavy attack from nature and survival meant reducing sail, which was far more important. All we had to do was get to any port alive and get off this wild ride to claim our prize, continued breathing.

"Dave! Come on. I need you up here!"

Nothing stirred from below. I jumped down off the lazarette, (the raised hatch cover over the stern storage locker) and moved as far forward as my extended arm would allow while still hanging onto the tiller.

I could hardly believe my eyes. The powerful, full-of-life, most outgoing guy in the world, Dave Hopkins, was slumped over the radio on the cabin floor holding his stomach. Had I not personally seen Dave go below I would have sworn I was ferrying a Gila monster. The combination of greenish, ashen face, once a rich bronze, cast an almost eerie glow throughout the cabin. I did not need another eerie event. Things were frightening enough.

"Are you alright?" I asked, already knowing the answer.

"How do I look?" came back the weak reply.

"You don't want to know. Get up here and into the air.

"I want to die. Leave me alone."

Seasickness can be the most debilitating sensation the ocean has to offer. Death is often a pleasant alternative. But while that may have been an appealing thought to Dave, in his crippled state, I needed him more than ever. My mind reeled. Unless I could get him functioning, I was really alone. It would be impossible to change the sails without him. And, if we did not change the sails soon, I feared the rigging would not take the strain. That activated images of the mast cracking and taking the whole boat down with it. I was scared out of my rain slicker. Alone on a stormy sea with little sailing experience and too much sail up, every fiber of my being wanted to get up and walk out of the theater to the peace and quiet of the lobby. I was trying hard not to bargain with God.

God, of course, seems to have the upper hand in this matter and, if there was a time for bargaining, now seemed like a good one. But something inside of me prevented those lengthy negotiations from beginning.. What if we did survive, then where would I be? No, bad as it was, I felt like Dave. Death was a better alternative. I was beginning to struggle as much with my inner self as much as the outer world.

What we both needed at this time was thinking and talking about something else. A diversion. The age old remedy for fear is denial. And, denial is best accomplished by chatter.

"Dave, try and get up here. I want to talk to you."

A minute passed and I thought he might have gone to sleep.

"What do you want to talk about?" he finally said.

"Oh, I don't know. How about the mainsail?"

"What about it?"

"We need to do *something*!"

"Take in a reef and call me in the morning." Dave said ever so slowly and without a trace of humor. He quite seriously did not want to be disturbed until morning. That, of course, left me where I started the conversation, nowhere.

A freak wave hit Nereus broadside. She shuddered and rolled heavily to port. I leaped back up on the lazarette and began working the boat through the next series of waves. Because the sea and sky were oven black, I literally could not see where the next wave was coming from until it was twenty feet off the bow. I danced us through one water wall after another, now thinking only about sailing.

I was so focused on my job that it almost startled me when Dave came up on deck. He held a safety harness in his right hand, and staggered back toward me, guided, no doubt, by the white incandescent glow of my knuckles. Without a word, he threw the belt around me nearly knocking me off my feet. He plunged the buckle into the lifeline and then helped me cinch up the straps around my middle. Without any response to my, "Thanks, I needed that," he moved forward to the cabin wall and sat down in a heap. While he sat recovering, I tried to figure out if he thoughtfully harnessed me to prevent my being swept overboard, which was a real possibility, or to prevent me from jumping overboard, which was not unthinkable.

Minutes passed before I whispered that I was very happy to see him. He nodded and I could see the color returning to his face.

"Do you have any idea what time it is?" I asked in an effort to generate conversation.

"9:45."

He sat there for another minute as I mulled over the implications of four hours of battling this storm and wondering if there were another four hours to go. Then, without a word, he leaped up and climbed along the weather side of the boat to the bow. The weather side of the boat meant the side facing the wind. It also meant that the sails were on the other side of the boat, the lee side, so that he was free from getting caught up in the rigging. But, at best, climbing along the narrow walkway leading to the bow was anything but easy. He made his way forward slowly and grabbed the mast.

"For Christ's sake; HANG ON!" I yelled. The thought of Dave slipping and going overboard was enough to turn my already overactive adrenaline output into mass production. I would never be able to turn Nereus around and even if I could I doubted very much that I would be able to find him in the heavy seas.

"You should be wearing this life line, not me!" I called again.

Dave grabbed the genny halyard, the line holding the genny up on the forestay, and began to unwrap it from the cleat. "I know!" I could hear him say over the roar of the wind. As he released the halyard, I uncleated the sheet, the line leading from the genny's bottom corner back to the cockpit winch. He let her down, gathering the resistant sail in his arms as it lowered chaotically. The deck was pitching wildly, exaggerated dramatically at the bow. Dave hung on with one hand to the bow pulpit and used the other to unhook the sail from the forestay. Meanwhile, I dug out the smaller jib and was prepared to push it forward when he was ready.

Dave's struggle defies accurate description. Twice he nearly went off the side as the bow burrowed into the sea. His fingers worked slowly in the cold water and the energy expended just to keep from falling overboard would have taxed Hercules, let alone someone recovering from seasickness. The genny, delivering so much power minutes before, now lay on the deck, a wet white nylon amoeba. He let the wind roll the limp sail back across the cabin top into my arms. I quickly stuffed the sail below and ushered up the jib.

In order for Dave to raise the sail, the boat had to be brought into the wind, taking all the pressure off the sails. It is tricky only to the extent that with no forward motion there is no rudder control and the boat can easily pick up on the wrong tack. This also has a tendency to knock the person on the bow clean into the water as the jib comes sweeping across the deck to join the main sails on the new tack. Just as Dave had the jib all set to be raised, Nereus did stall and fall off on a port tack. With the sail still on the deck nothing happened to Dave, but in the cockpit, I was ducking my head with vigor as the boom came zipping across the stern nearly clobbering me.

"Hang on. I'll bring her back on course in a second!"

But I was unable to bring her around on the first try. It was simply a matter of not having enough speed. In order not to have to jibe, that is, come all the way around, in these heavy seas, I let Nereus fall way off and with the help of the next passing wave, jerked the tiller over as the boat started to fall into the trough. The speed of the fall, added to that of the wind, brought her around sharply. Dave was hanging on for dear life throughout this maneuvering and gave me a thumbs-up when we were set right again. Then he quickly hauled in the halyard, sending the jib up the forestay. The ship was turned into the wind for a moment, both sails flapping violently back and forth in a complete stall position. The second I tightened down on the jib sheet, wound around the starboard winch, and put the tiller down, Nereus sprang forward.

We were now running with a smaller sail up front. With her new sail combination, she ran much easier. If we had been able to make the proper adjustments when we saw the storm coming we would have avoided much of the last hour's nightmare. Since we'd never tried to reef the main before, especially in heavy seas, I was praying the wind would not pick up anymore. The storm raged on—no better, no worse.

While I stood in silence at the tiller, almost fearing that mere speech would further upset the balance of nature, Dave chatted on like a drunken sailor. It was becoming clear that our individual method for handling anxiety was antithetical. When I am in a tight spot and wringing wet with perspiration and fear, silence is my defense. Everything is focused and internal for me. To others, I must appear stoic, masterful or catatonic. On the other hand, Dave's anxiety management system employed verbiage and lots of it. He rattles on about anything and everything. And being a professor, there is lots for him to rattle on about.

No doubt part of the fault was mine. He must have been trying, at some point, to determine whether my silence was the heroic type or the catatonic type. Since I was silent, I, of course, was of no help and he was forced to talk all the more. Dave's monologue could have gone on for some time had his next question not brought me to immediate conversation.

"Did you hear that?"

Expecting to hear the hull cracking apart or the rigging snapping under the strain of the storm, I listened intently for half a second and looked to him for explanation.

"Other than the wind and waves and my heart, I don't hear anything I'm not supposed to. What is it?" I said.

"Listen, there it is again. Someone just slammed a door."

"Right."

"I'll let you know if I hear it again."

"Do that," I said with concealed concern. Seasickness can be more damaging than I thought.

But I had not thought that long for, as I listening for a door to slam, I looked out on the water and saw sheep running across the waves.

"There, did you see that?" I jabbed at Dave, pointing in the direction of the last sighted sheep.

He played the, "No, what are you talking about?" game for a bit until *he* saw something that looked like a sheep run across the water.

"Ok, I saw it, but it wasn't a sheep. It was the white foam streaking down the face of the wave that makes the sheep-like appearance on the water."

But when Dave thought he heard *another* door slam and someone say, "Hello", I thought it was time we stopped this madness before we got too carried away. Tired eyes and tired ears play funny tricks in the disorienting atmosphere of night sailing. Here we were only half way through the night and both a little flaky. Can you imagine what happens to solo sailors trying to circumnavigate the world?

By 11:30 p.m. I was totally exhausted. The wind had abated considerably and we were sailing along at four knots riding the waves with greater ease. Dave had long since recovered and was more than willing to take the tiller for a spell. Things seemed to be much more under control. I was relaxing again and sleep sounded like a sojourn to Nirvana. I unhooked my lifeline and with all the pomp and pageantry the changing of the watch merited, I passed the gear over to him. A few comments were exchanged and I set off through the companionway for a soft cushioned bunk below. I went down the one step ladder, into the darkness, and… four-inches of water.

"C-C-Christ!! Dave, we're sinking!"

Without a word, Dave was through the companionway and digging for the hand pump. I flew out of the cabin and grabbed the deserted tiller. In case of emergency, as we had carefully theorized, on the way down, I would man the tiller and prepare the life raft for use. Dave was to go below and either fix the problem, if it was fixable, or dig out the survival box filled with water, food, flare guns, etc.

"Go forward and turn on the bilge pump." I yelled. "It's the top switch on the control panel."

Dave scrambled forward in the dark and flipped the switch. Over the next several minutes, we noticed that the two carefully installed bilge pumps managed to spit out maybe a teaspoon of water. Whether the pumps weren't primed or just didn't work, we never determined. Dave shut them down and grabbed the more reliable hand pump. Within fifteen minutes he had pumped the cabin relatively dry. He ejected the soaking rug, picked up the various goods that had not been successfully battened down and began to look for the cause of the leak.

"There doesn't seem to be any more water coming in. I'll check around and see if I can find out where all this water was coming from."

I stood at the tiller, steering in the lessening but still active storm, figuratively holding my breath. I could see him moving about the cabin, checking under bunks and seats, lifting up cushions and covers and inspecting the vee berth. Then I lost sight of him as he began pulling out our carefully stowed boxes under the cockpit. For what seemed like an eternity, I could hear him maneuvering around in the tight quarters under my feet. Finally, he poked his head over the companionway step.

"You're not going to believe this."

"Try me."

"Which do you want first, the good news or the bad?"

"Give me the bad."

"We've lost all our fresh water."

With my active imagination, I assumed the stern had been torn away, that we were sinking, and that the fresh water bag had been ripped out through the undoubtedly large hole in our hull. Well, at that rate, I thought we wouldn't need the fresh water anyway, so that wasn't so bad. I'm cool. I'd just wait here at the tiller until the ship goes down. I continued to mentally play out macabre scenarios until Dave finally reappeared and rushed into the whole story.

Apparently, during the worst part of the storm, the crashing and banging around was too much for the water bag, wedged between containers that no doubt took the opportunity to throw their weight around. The pressure caused the hose to separate from the bag and allowed all our water to flood the cabin floor.

"Well, how do *you* spell relief?" I finally said, after the impact of our good luck settled in. For the first time on this 'New York Post' experience, we both laughed. The tension broke and even though little had changed weather-wise, we could feel the wind beginning to lessen and the seas starting to settle down.

75

Half-off Sail

I finally retired below, tired, but in improved spirits. Even picking up the few renegade cans of Beef with Barley, Split Pea, and Tomato with Rice did not bother me much. The lower food locker in the vee berth had popped open again and sent most of its contents flying. But Nereus had never been heavy weather tested and these minor problems seemed quite manageable. It was during this first venture into the cabin during heavy seas that introduced me to an aspect of sailing that I had never, up to now, experienced.

On deck there is comparatively a great deal of room to catch one's balance as the boat tosses you around from tiller to post. Below, it is a different story. You can't see when or even where the next wave is going to hit. Caught unaware, you are suddenly propelled into the nearest stationary object.

But your perception isn't that you lost *your* balance and hit them. It becomes more personal. It's as if they came out and hit you. Just getting from the companionway to the vee berth forced a physically encounter with a butcher block table, a galley, the bulkhead dividing the cabin and the above-mentioned assortment of canned goods. By the time I reached the berth, well battered, I found that I had cursed everything in my path and personally challenged the butcher block table to a duel. I did, however, finally manage to dive into the berth and assuage my aching head by letting it come to rest on the "forward state room" pillow. I had managed to shed my foul weather gear before climbing into bed but slept fully clothed, ready to spring into action should there be a need. I could have dressed in my pajamas as it turned out. Within minutes, I was soundly in a dreamless sleep and lost to the next four hours.

The next sound I heard was a soft spoken, "Bob, can you come on deck?" I grabbed a flashlight and was up and through the forward hatch in two seconds flat. I raced back to the cockpit, and, without even thinking, aimed the light at the compass. We were on course; the sails were fine, but not very full, and all was in order.

"Problems?" I asked with a note of concern.

"Well, yes. I'm falling asleep and it is *your* watch."

"Any real problems?"

"No, except for the fact that I turned north for about an hour. I thought we had sailed too far east during the storm and just made that minor mid-course correction."

With that summary, Dave retired and I took command. It was a totally different scene this time. The Nereus was sailing through gently rolling seas at three knots. The sky looked like someone had thrown a thousand diamonds against black silk. The sparkle was magnificent. And the stern turned up the most interesting phosphorescent shapes in the sea. Each was different and totally shapeless. I sailed with ease in the Epicurean night. The water hissed under the hull, the white foam boiled out from the bow and it was almost like being in a dream-like state.

The sails began to flap, the boat stood still for a moment ... and we stalled out. I *was* in a dream state! I had fallen asleep at the tiller! I snapped my head up, corrected the course and for a time, brought the boat back on track. But within short order I drifted off again. The sails flapped and I had to snap my head back to bring myself fully awake. I tried several more times, but simply did not have it in me. Whatever energy I expended during the storm had taken its toll and I was not fit for piloting.

"Dave." I called in almost a whisper, hoping he was wide awake and my call wouldn't be an intrusion. Nothing.

"Dave, can you come on deck?" I called in a louder voice. Just like me he was on deck in two seconds flat, slightly out of breath, asking for details of the problem. When I told him there was no problem other than the fact that I was exhausted, he disappeared below for a minute and then came up chuckling.

"Do you know what time it is?"

"Not really. I figure it will be dawn any minute now and you should take the tiller."

"Now, don't get upset, but it's only 1:30 in the morning. You've been at the tiller no more than an hour!"

It is to Dave's everlasting credit and my everlasting embarrassment, that with only one comment to the effect that he'd been on for four hours and off one, he took command and I fell back into the vee berth.

The sun had broken across the empty sea when I finally came on deck. It was about 6:00 a.m. and I had a good night's sleep behind me. Dave, on the other hand, was not in the best of spirits.

"Enjoy your sleep, you pampered swabby?"

Without responding to the obvious dig, I looked around. The entire scene had changed. The sea was a giant millpond, flat as a dark blue linoleum floor. The sails hung limp and Dave's right arm hung casually over the unresponsive tiller. The light blue sky supported puffy white clouds forty thousand feet in the air. Nothing moved. Not the wind. Not the sea. And certainly not us.

"What's happening out here?" I began.

"Christ, I'm no climatologist! The wind dropped off at 4:00 a.m. and what you see is what we've got."

By all calculations, we should have been nearing West End in the Bahamas. We had been sailing roughly thirteen hours, and at worst, the sixty mile voyage, averaging three miles an hour, (forget about 'knots') should have taken us twenty hours. Right? Then add to that the fact that we had been clipping along at five and six knots most of the night, at least that part of the night I could remember, would put us very near our goal. At worst, we could motor the rest of the way. The main thing now was to get back to Dave's original problem. We needed to know where the blazes we were.

"Well, maybe we can figure out where we are after some coffee and breakfast. I'll take the tiller forever if you want to fix some grits. On the other hand, I owe you a big one for last night and if you want me to fix the food, I'll be happy to do it."

"No, you go ahead and steer for a while. I need a change. And besides, I'm better at boiling water than you are."

It was true. I couldn't cook my way out of an instant Cup-of-Soup. So with a quick change in seat assignments, Dave went below to start the water and rustle up some *good* food. We were both near starvation. Have you ever been so hungry you can taste bacon long before it's cooking? I was sure that within minutes, some culinary delight would be presented. What actually arrived, not too many minutes later, was that good coffee and cocoa, but also a hand full of peanuts, raisins and some cookies.

"Sorry about the menu, but I just don't have it in me to make eggs Benedict this morning."

I, of course, had nothing to complain about. Sleep and hot coffee in the early lovely morning at sea was plenty. The peanuts, raisins and cookies were okay too. It was so peaceful, majestic, silent and tranquil.

Dave futzed around the cabin for a while, cleaning up odds and ends that had launched themselves around the ship during the night. By 7 a.m., or so, he called out that he would try and get some idea as to where, on this vast ocean, we were. For the next half hour, I could hear the radio chatter and pages of the navigational guide book flipping back and forth. It was so peaceful and so beautiful on this, our first morning on the open ocean, that I paid Dave's navigational exercise scant attention.

My reverie declined markedly when Dave came on deck with a coffee cup in hand and sat down to begin the morning briefing.

"If that thing in there (referring to the RDF) is even close to right, we are in deep shit. There was no signal from West End. The strongest signal came from Jupiter. I picked up signals, weak as could be, from Hillsboro and then something way up the coast. The little hat all those lines make on the chart places us about twenty miles off the northern coast of Florida!"

My jaw nearly put a hole through the deck as it dropped open. "The northern coast of Florida!? You can't be serious!?" But I could tell he was only too serious.

"If that's true, and I can check it again, there is no way we can get back to West End. "Here," Dave dragged out the chart and began stabbing his finger at radio beacons, current positions and the Brahma Bank. "Even if we try and make a run for the Bank, I would guess, from this position, we are at least 55 miles away—assuming there's no current. Add all that up, and I can't see how we would even have a prayer of hitting the Bank on the northern tip, let alone the middle, from this angle."

79

"And, God forbid we miss the northern tip. We would be headed for Greenland."

"Right," Dave agreed despondently.

"All of which means we missed our island and have no choice but to turn back for Florida. And, if we turn back for Florida, we just blew our trip," I said in a mood of black, flooding despair. It was as if someone pulled a plug on my unconditional positive response reserve tank.

"Now, hold on just a second. We don't know that yet. I think we've got to turn back to the coast. But let's get there, wherever there is, and see what happens. We may be in great shape for another try."

"Do you really believe that?"

"No, but it sounds like the only way of managing our decision."

"Right. Well, I'll bring her about and let's check our position in an hour or so and see if we can get a sense of where we'll spend the night in Florida."

The Nereus came around ever so slowly in the nonexistent wind. She seemed as reluctant as we to give up the dream. We headed for the Florida coast at a snail's pace. The self-imposed hour limit on our run, before a position check, left us with little to do but occasionally trim the deflated sails and clean up.

To counteract the dramatic current of the Gulf Stream, I sailed a course of 240 degrees hoping to get out of the main flow as quickly as possible, yet sail west. We knew that the further north we drifted the longer the trip back to the car would be. Dave had set up the course in the hopes of landing in West Palm Beach. He had checked the Inland Waterways Guide and determined that if we could make that, we had roughly a two-day trip back. So, for the moment, although we had failed to reach our goal, we had survived the night, the storm, and were at least on our way...*somewhere*.

At 8:45 a.m., Dave went below to make a progress report. Within ten minutes he was back on deck. "We're in trouble," he reported.

My blood turned cold and what he proceeded to tell me chilled it even further.

"This goddamn current is something else. Not only have we made no progress, we've actually been swept out to sea. Here, look." Again, Dave had the chart in front of me and without his telling me and I could see that the little hat that brought all the lines together had our position north and slightly to the east of his first reading.

"Jesus, we *are* being swept out to sea. We've got to start the engine or we'll be drifting into the mid-Atlantic by noon!"

There was no point in discussing the issue. I turned the tiller over to Dave and began the arm-demolishing task of starting the engine. This day was no different than any other day for that incorrigible piece of debris we called an engine. By my traditional thirtieth pull on the starter cord, I heated myself and the engine up enough so that she was forced to sputter into life. I collapsed and muttered incoherently for a good ten minutes after the ordeal. "Someday I gotta fix that damn thing," was about the only thing I could say that Dave understood.

Dave corrected the course so we were pointed further south and we began the long motor trip back. I am foursquare against humiliation. But how humiliating. Not only did we not make our island dream, but we had to motor our stout little *sailing* ship to boot. Our only hope now was to avoid the press. The 'I-told-you-so' group would have a field day with the news.

The midmorning sun provided the first typical Floridian day since our arrival: extreme heat, humidity and no wind. Hats were jammed in place; liberal doses of sunscreen and long-sleeved shirts made up the morning costume. To get out of the beating rays, we took turns in the cabin either reorganizing the disrupted gear from our pell-mell ride the night before, or just resting. Rest was needed, but not easily accomplished knowing that an unwanted adventure into the Atlantic was being prevented, at this moment, by our little seven-horsepower Gamefisher Sears engine. I was listening to every revolution of the engine for that feared cough or sputter. The slightest sneeze could put us adrift into the vast Atlantic and

Half-off Sail

back in the soup. Our track record for getting into *the soup* was pretty good so far, and extra vigilance was required.

We motored and occasionally commented about the blistering heat, and we motored some more. But when Dave started reciting chapter and verse from the "Rhyme of the Ancient Mariner", I decided that we needed to refocus our attention. Since I was below at the time of his theatrics, I grabbed the trusty binoculars and pounced on deck with the enthusiastic announcement that land was certainly in sight by now, and I would go forward to confirm our position. To no one's surprise, land was not in sight. However, something else was and I called back my findings.

"There's a tanker about two miles ahead off the port bow. Check the chart and see if there are any identified shipping lanes. They might give us a clue as to where we are."

Dave, now considerably more focused, pulled the chart from under a seat cushion and from what I could tell from between looking at him and looking at the ship (as if it would disappear), he was coming up with something.

"If I'm reading this thing right, it looks like they have two shipping lanes out here. The closer one is about seven miles off the coast. The other one is pretty far out."

"Let's take the closer one!" I called back.

"Ok. We could use a little delusional boost."

We motored on for another two uneventful hours. The coastline was becoming more visible, but there were no identifiable markers to give us even the vaguest hint as to where we were. And, lacking that knowledge, we really did not know whether we should be turning north to make port, go further south or just staying on our present course.

We needed some guidance badly. Of course, we couldn't ask anyone for help over the radio since we didn't know where we were. So, we just kept motoring and hoping for some hint. It came at 2:30 in the afternoon. "Look!" cried Dave. "Over there. About two points off the port bow!" In the distance was the object of Dave's excitement. There, visible to the engaged yachtsman, about a mile away, was a boat motoring at about 8 knots or so, heading out to sea.

"We have to get their attention!" I shouted. I elaborated further by suggesting we set the sails on fire. Dave rejected that plan and came up with a more sensible approach. "Go below and get out the mirror. We can signal him and then get on the radio." I think his suggestion was followed by some form of address like "asshole", but I was digging into the lockers for the mirror and really didn't hear whatever he said. Once on deck, I caught the sun in the mirror and flashed continuously. Dave went below and gave our relative position, by radio, which included something about a yellow sail boat with two maniacal guys running around on deck, just off his starboard bow.

The call was returned several minutes later, the delay, no doubt, a factor of the entire crew trying to determine if we needed a tow or not. A tow would certainly have destroyed their plans for the day and understandably, they did not want to get involved. But Dave had apparently given the proper reassurance that our primary need was for direction.

The 30-foot fishing boat maneuvered alongside in the next several minutes and the thoughts among the four retired New Yorker types peering over the rail can only be imagined.

"You folks just need directions?" came the apprehensive reconfirmation from the skipper. Charts came out and several helpful comments followed. It seemed that we were about four miles off shore and the closest port of any consequence was Saint Lucie's Inlet, a total of about seven miles to the harbor entrance.

After all our wanderings, seven miles to safety didn't seem all that bad. What was bad was the fact that promptly following the report of our position and a compass bearing designed to get us into the harbor, the skipper put down both throttles of his twin 250's and roared away. Granted, he had a right to do that since it was his boat and he most probably had paying customers aboard. But, the flamboyant display of power was a bit much not to mention the fact that we weren't even offered a cold beer. I asked myself, who, in all the world, especially on this oceanic desert, looked like they needed a beer, a cold beer, more than the two of us?

Nevertheless, we had something almost as valuable as cold beer. We basically knew where the hell we were and basically where we should be going to get out of this mess. Just four short miles away was the blessed coast of Florida and, not all that far beyond was the Inlet at Saint Lucie's. Things couldn't be all that bad. We were going to survive this ordeal after all.

Land soon came more clearly into view. Each revolution of the engine pushed us just that much closer to our goal. My apprehensive focus on the engine diminished proportionately to our distance from the shore, which was getting closer all the time. But we were clearly being pushed north by the Gulf Stream and we still had "miles to go before we slept."

"Let's get as close to the shore as possible. The current has to be less forceful closer in and we can motor down the coast to get to the Inlet," I said, with all due respect to the offending current. Dave agreed and shifted direction ever so slightly to get us more on a direct line to the shore. With three miles to go, Dave went below and got on the radio. "This is Whiskey Alpha Poppa, 3303, calling the Coast Guard Station at Jupiter Inlet. Come in please. Over."

'Whiskey Alpha Poppa, 3303?' Where in the world did that come from? I wondered alone because Dave remained below in what sounded like an argument for another couple of minutes.

When he reappeared, I stopped him half way through the companionway with two questions: "What was that all about and where did this 'Whiskey Alpha Poppa, 3303' come from?"

"Those Coast Guard guys think that Saint Lucie's Inlet is dangerous and suggested we go sixteen miles north to Fort Pierce. Can you imagine? They must be nuts!" was his reply.

"Yeah, *they* are nuts. How much of the story did you tell them?"

"Most of it. Why?"

"Christ. No wonder they thought *we* were nuts. But where did this 'Whiskey Alpha Poppa, 3303' come from?"

Dave grinned. "You know we never got that radio registered and if I'm calling the Coast Guard station, I sure as hell want to do it with some degree of formality. I made it up. God knows we've broken every other rule of boating."

I thought about this for a minute and decided he wasn't nearly as dumb as our circumstance indicated. "True. So, what do you think?"

"What do you mean, 'What do I think?' You know what I think. We have to head down to Saint Lucie's. We certainly don't have the energy or the fuel to motor up to Fort Pierce."

"Right," I said. "Just checking. I mean, forget the fact that there are a series of 'S' turns that are dangerous. And forget about the fact that we are underpowered and don't know the harbor. We have to do it." And, with that we both fell silent, knowing that there was little more to discuss. It was 4:15 p.m.

Without warning, the engine roared into overdrive and began shaking like a martini shaker full of ice. I flew to the engine, almost as if prepared, and shut it down with lightning speed. But not fast enough.

I looked over the transom and saw what I feared I might see. The engine was shut down, supposedly in gear (since I didn't have time to flip her into neutral) and there was the propeller spinning free as a bird. There was a bulge of bluish metal half way down the shaft, just above the waterline. Before I could really think through what had happened, I knew exactly what it was. The propeller shaft was broken. I didn't know why but I just hung over the stern in silence trying to let reality surface through my profound defense of denial.

It was when Dave said, ever so quietly, "Bad?" that I brought myself back and into the present.

"Bad! The engine is gone. Can you think of anything worse?"

We both sat there numb. Playing out the worst case scenario, we had a first-class disaster on our hands. Off shore, at dusk, in alien waters, with no power, trying to get into a "dangerous inlet," at best, had all the makings for death and destruction. Piled up on some lonely beach was the good side of the equation. Drifting aimlessly out to sea was... well... nothing to dwell on.

As Chief Officer in Charge of Engine Maintenance, I was duty bound to at least examine the causality and pronounce the final diagnosis. While Dave silently took the tiller, I once again leaned over the transom, disconnected the fuel line, dragged the engine up the resistant track and unscrewed the wing nuts holding our cripple at her former duty station. With a heave-ho, I brought the wreck over the side and into the cockpit. Sure enough, one look told the story. Her shaft was broken. The propeller spun freely to my touch and the casing around the vertical shaft bulged in all the wrong places. My only thoughts were how to rig some sort of proper burial to show our last respects for the little engine that had tried so hard and brought us so close.

"Well, now what?" I said despondently.

Dave thought for a moment, "Perhaps we can sail in."

I had not noticed, in my preoccupation with the disaster, that the Nereus was actually sailing along at some two to three knots. I promptly upgraded our situation from disaster to merely dismal. Here was a new hope I had not thought of. We might be able to sail in.

"Check the tide charts and see if the gods have stopped laughing long enough to have the tide going in," I said with a slightly upbeat tone. I took the tiller, while Dave went below, and let my sweaty palm gently ease the tiller back and forth bringing the Nereus into her best sailing position. When Dave called up a few minutes later with the news that, contrary to all our past hours of experience, we *did* have the blessing of the gods with a returning tide, the situation was again upgraded from dismal to "we might live"

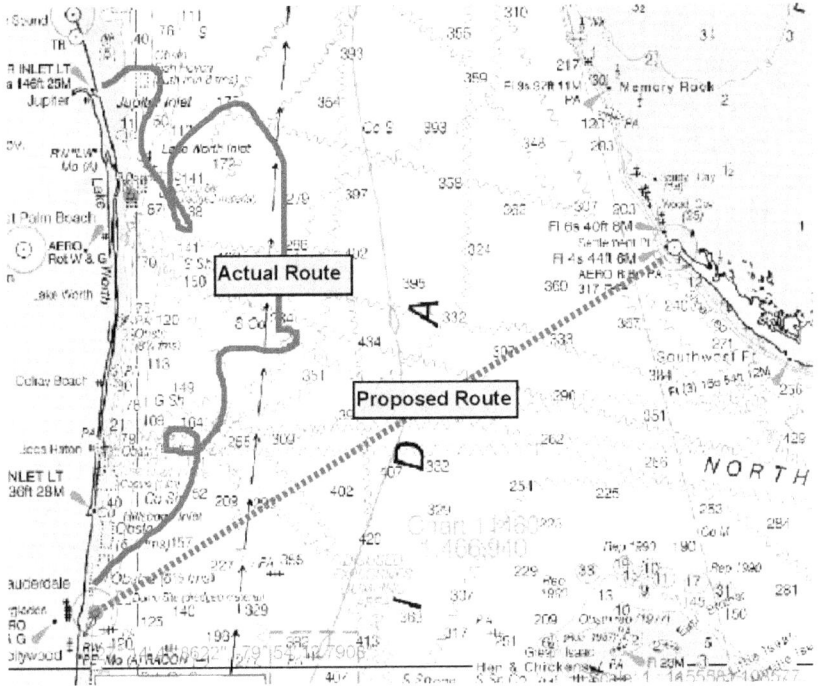

Saint Lucie's Inlet was now only a mile ahead. We could see the narrow rocky opening. Having never sailed into a harbor before (we had always motored in), this was going to be tricky, at best.

We were so close to safety, yet fickle currents, hidden rocks and rudimentary charts made our chances for successful entry relatively low by most insurance company standards. I could just picture some claims agent trying to get a clear picture of the events that let up to our piling the Nereus up on the foreboding rocks ahead. 'What do you mean you just tried to sail in? The Coast Guard told you not to try it, right? Well, what the hell were you two guys thinking of?'

We were thinking of a lot as we rounded the inlet entrance. Dave had raced forward to direct our movements from the vantage point of the bow. I was standing at the tiller now, rather than sitting. Gear, loosely piled on deck during our long motor, had hurriedly been thrown below. And, the engine, who had given her all, had been shifted out of the way.

"Follow my directions closely!" Dave called from the bow.

Half-off Sail

He had a crude copy of the harbor entrance chart in hand and would pilot us in, to the best of his ability, using mostly his observations. Since there was a white cloud of canvas blocking most of my view, I couldn't have hoped for more.

"Right!" But make 'em clear." I went forward and cranked up the centerboard allowing Nereus to draw only eighteen inches of water. The rope that held the lower unit of the rudder in the down position was loosened, but not freed. If worse came to worse and we ran aground, I wanted to be able to have that rudder up and out of the way quickly.

We had two things going for us now—the tide and the wind. The channel entrance came up fast. Before we knew it we were sweeping past the first part of the breakwater and into the channel itself. Our concentration was intense, and we could have passed dead bodies in the water without noticing.

We were really moving by the time we entered the end of the breakwater. With the wind almost directly at our backs, and the four-knot current, the paralleling shoreline made us feel like we were going sixty. No doubt the long hours of no reference points made the rapidly passing markers overly dramatic but whatever it was, we were moving. With the wind and current running in the same direction, there was little chop on the swirling channel water. I could see Dave standing on the bow, looking ahead intently, his hand poised and ready for split-second directions. I bounced from side to side in the cockpit, trying to gain better visual contact with everything ahead. I could see a rocky shoreline dead ahead and tried desperately to wait out Dave's signal for a turn. It looked like it was getting very close to the point of no return.

"Don't wait too long!" I called. "The current will sweep us past the marker!"

Dave hung on to his directions. Another few seconds passed and he shouted, "Now!"

I jammed the tiller to the port and the bow swung sharply to starboard. I sheeted in both the main and the genny, brought the tiller back to mid-ship and checked with Dave for accuracy of the maneuver. He was pointing one point off the port bow and I made the minor correction. He flashed an "OK" sign and we were steady as she goes. As the mouth of the inlet widened, the current lessened and our speed fell off to three knots. Another buoy was coming up and I made ready.

"This turn will take us back around the opposite way. Get ready to come about with the sails. Will you need a hand?"

"No!" I called back. "Just keep me on course and if you can, walk the genny over."

In the light wind and with reduced speed, we were going to need every assist possible, and Dave literally carrying the big front sail from one side of the boat to the other would help. He put down his near worthless chart and readied for the maneuver. In very short order, he called to come about and a flurry of activity erupted on deck for the change. We were going to gybe this one. The main would come cracking around with the wind taking hold of her from behind. I snugged down the mainsheet to prevent too much play in the boom. I threw the tiller over. She sent a sharp crack through the air as the sail came across the deck and filled again on the starboard side. Dave had the genny muscled around the mast and I sheeted her in quickly. Seconds later we were clipping along in the opposite direction. And not more than thirty seconds later Dave was calling for another change, sending us back again in almost the opposite course. We jockeyed around through the series of 'S' turns for another few minutes and made it through the last buoy. We were safe!

We were drifting smoothly on the quiet lagoon of Saint Lucie's Bay. The current slowly died and the wind became a whisper as we deepened our way into the backwater. Ahead was a marina and we prepared to lower the sails. The dock was still some distance away but getting closer. I left the tiller and sprang to the mast where I released the main sail halyard. Together we lashed the sail to the boom and let the genny slowly tow us to the dock. With only twenty feet to go, Dave dropped the genny and stowed it on the deck. I rummaged around the stern locker for dock lines and threw him two coils, saving the last one for the stern. With only four feet to go, Dave leaped from the bow onto the dock and guided the boat gently alongside the slip. With our position set, we tied off the lines and placed the bumpers in strategic spots. I stood up and wearily looked around. It was amazing and I was awestruck.

"You fellas come far?" called out a voice from a nearby boat.

Dave and I looked at each other. He turned to the man who appeared to be in his late fifties and said, "Not as far as we wanted, but farther than we expected."

"Want a cold beer?" he said. Dave and I traded smirks then returned "aye captain."

BROKEN PARTS AND BROKEN HEARTS

The pastoral waterfront vista should have had us managing a serious case of euphoria. We were surrounded by small parks dotted with trees and palms, flat blue water, clear warm skies and a secure dock. But we were anything but euphoric. After an attempt to regroup, the suggestion was made that we resume our traditional method of crisis management by strolling to the nearest liquor store. Within a few minutes we were making the mile hike to the nearest provider of liquid relief.

It's always interesting to see what one reaches for when trying to resolve a crisis. And it would be of interest to some advertising agency to know that what we reached for was a six-pack of 16 ounce cans of Bush Bavarian Beer with its' picture of clear blue skies and snow-covered mountains. The can alone looked refreshing. Forget the quality of the contents. Just drink and look at the picture, that's what we did. By the time we reached the Nereus we had consumed four of the six cans and were feeling much better. But not good enough to encourage unconditional positive thinking. I seemed more depressed than Dave, who was himself withdrawn and uncharacteristically quiet. I opened the conversation with one of my more positive thoughts. "Shall we sell her?" The words almost stuck in my throat. So much time, money and love had gone into this dream. The countless evenings of work, the schooling, the training, the reading, the trials and the promise of it all streamed across my mind. The idea was obviously too overwhelming since I did not even acknowledge Dave's, "That's a good idea." Again, with my facility for denial operating at maximum efficiency, I continued to make incredibly unrealistic suggestions. Dave fielded each one with surgical accuracy, zeroing in on the impractical nature of each.

"What about trying to sail her down the coast and at least get her back to the car?"

After rolling his eyes back into identifiably human positions, Dave proceeded to ask a series of questions that made the answer to my suggestions all too obvious. "Do you really want to go back out on the Atlantic with the unpredictable winds, fighting the Gulf Stream all the way to Hillsboro with no engine?" To respond to this line of reasoning seemed superfluous, so instead, I offered more suggestions.

"Perhaps one of us could hitch hike to the car and drive it back up here with the trailer."

"You realize, of course, that the battery to the car is in the boat, with us, and one of us would have to make a sixty-mile thumb journey with battery in hand."

"We could just leave her and call the insurance company," I offered.

"They don't settle claims without a body," Dave said smoothly while popping the top to our last can of beer. The conversation, continued in this depressing vein. I offered suggestions such as going down to the Keys or perhaps even rowing down the Inland Water Way until the sun painted a bright red line across the horizon. Somehow, with no clear resolution to our problem, the conversation turned to a more practical subject: dinner. It had been over thirty hours since we had had a good meal and the thought of food suddenly lifted the gloom. The galley came alive and Dave began to work his culinary magic: Libby's Beef Stew with mixed veggies, covered with a liberal dose of Kraft cheese from a pressurized can washed down with two mugs full of gin and tonic. It was just what Dugan would have recommended in his famous nautical book, *Survive the Savage Sea*.

The brilliant sunset trailed a blanket of darkness behind its western descent and a show of stars began to twinkle, making everything seem small in the greater scheme. Here we were struggling to get sixty miles across the sea, delighted to make even three knots, when men were launching planetary probes that traveled at 40,400 miles per hour, millions upon millions of miles across the heavens. How strange it all seemed. Our struggle seemed so pedestrian. Yet it was the most real thing I had ever encountered.

Neil Diamond's album "Hot August Night" played in the background while we talked the evening away. We talked of our journey and our adventure, we talked about home and women. We had another drink then we went off to our different corners of the boat to sleep. Tomorrow would have to solve today's problems. *Carpe Mañana* was the philosophy. Thoughts of the future just weren't what they used to be.

The sun came through the forward hatch at 6:00 a.m. I rolled over in my little stateroom, comforted by being surrounded by my own handiwork and slept until seven. I awoke to the sound of Dave cleaning up the cabin and could have dozed off for another hour when I heard a voice call out a cheery greeting to Dave.

"Good morning in there!" Dave popped up and returned the bidding. "My name is Rick and I like to think of myself as the Dockmaster," the voice said. "How long will y'all be stay'n with us?"

I could hear Dave clear his throat and give a long, "We-l-l-l...", followed by a brief summary of our tale. I poked my head through the hatch and focused on the smooth-faced 'kid' whose mouth was slightly agape as he listened to the story.

"...so, if we could stay for a couple of days," Dave was concluding, "we can figure out how to get out of this mess."

If the Royal Society on Human Kindness had schooled Rick, it couldn't have done a finer job.

"No problem," Rick began. "Just pull the boat over to the far dock there. You'll be out of the way of our impatient senior citizens, itching to gas up their jet boats. John, the mechanic, sometimes gets in by nine o'clock. You can bring that engine up to him and see if there is anything he can do." Inanimate objects in the boat couldn't get out of my way quickly enough as I broiled through the bulkhead door, past the mostly clean galley and on up through the companionway. I rushed past Dave, leaped up on the dock and began vigorously pumping Rick's hand, which was not yet fully extended due to the surprise meeting.

"Goddamnit!! You have wonderful thoughts for this hour of the morning. Good morning to you! I'm Bob, the guy Dave was telling you about who got us into this mess," I said to his apparent amusement.

By nine o'clock the boat was cleaned from bow to stern and I was lugging our wounded engine up to the repair shop. The rest of our trip depended on John the mechanic's diagnosis, and we stood with anxiously thumping hearts as he turned his professional eyes on her. In thirty seconds we had our answer. There was no way he could fix the Sear's Gamefisher engine.

"And, what were you guys doing out in the Atlantic with this thing, anyway?"

"It's all we could afford," I offered with less than overbearing confidence.

"Well, the best you can do now is take it back."

"I'm afraid we bought this thing in New Jersey, so 'taking it back' might be a little difficult right now," Dave added in a resigned monotone.

John brought his shoulders up to his ears, raised his hands slightly upward and nonverbally indicated there was nothing more he could do. We picked up the engine, retraced our steps to the boat and climbed back aboard to fix coffee and to think out our next step. We postponed our discussion until our second cup.

"Now what?" I ventured.

"I don't know. Do you think there's a Sear's store around here?" Dave casually wondered.

"Jesus! I must have my brains in my tennis shoes. Of course. That's a great idea." There was a pause in my jubilation as I returned to the practical side of the problem. "But where and who would know?"

"Rick."

"Right again. Boy, they didn't give you a Doctorate for noth'in. Let's go ask him."

So, with mugs in hand, we strolled around the boat yard looking for Rick. We found him in one of the big sheds, and after politely waiting for him to finish talking with a paying customer -one can never be too polite when one is in a jam with little or no money- the story unfolded followed by our simple question.

"Sure. West Palm has a huge Sear's store."

"Great!" I said. "How far is West Palm?"

"Thirty-five miles or so."

"How far?" I squeaked, envisioning hitch hiking with a heavy engine on a 70 mile round trip.

"Take my car," Rick said without batting an eye. I knew what Dave was thinking when we both looked at each other in amazement. Would you loan your car to two guys sailing a small boat in the Atlantic with a Sears Gamefisher engine for power? John had been the first person to certify us as nuts, and there were undoubtedly legions of folk all too ready with the same conclusion. But, here was Rick offering us dock space, engine help and now his car.

"Just go down, get your engine and take it to the parking lot. My car is the light blue station wagon at the far end—the keys are under the mat."

Unbelievable!!

Dave and I were halfway out the door as we called out our thanks.

We ran down the dock with Dave in the lead and leaped into the cockpit, he to wrestle the engine up to the dock and me to quickly gather my wallet, checkbook, sunglasses and windbreaker. It was assumed that I would make the journey given the fact that I was in charge of engine maintenance.

"I don't know how long I'll be, but as soon as I find out something, I'll give you a call at Rick's office," I said, out of breath.

I grabbed the engine and lumbered back up the dock for the second time. I wanted to get going before Rick thought better of his generosity. The car was not quite where I thought it would be, from Rick's description, but it was the right color, a station wagon, and sure enough, the keys were under the mat. I ran around to the tailgate, unlocked the door, threw in the engine, slammed the gate shut, leaped into the driver's seat and plugged the key into the ignition, eager to get out of recall distance. I turned the key..., and sat back in disbelief. Absolutely nothing happened when I turned the key. So it was a joke after all. Was it fair for this to be happening to me? Surely the gods had laughed themselves sick the day before; they shouldn't have the strength to enjoy an instant replay. I tried it again, only to realize that fair or not, it really was happening. The engine didn't even grunt. I climbed slowly back out and trudged back up to the office.

"Rick, when was the last time you ran your car?" I said, halfway through the front door.

"This morning. Why?" He said sitting straight up in his seat.

"Well, is the sun particularly hard on batteries down here?"

"No, but it can fade paint. Let's go have a look."

Walking toward the parking lot Rick kept angling off to the left while I was headed in a straight line. Finally, I asked him where he was going.

"To my car. Where the hell are you going?"

It was like someone had plugged my finger into a light socket. My God! I had the wrong car. The mental image of driving down the highway, being pulled over by the state police and arrested for grand theft auto flashed across my mind. 'Did you fix the engine, Bob?' 'No, I'm in Jail' would have concluded the day's conversation.

What was going through Rick's mind is hard to guess. The engine was switched from the identical color Ford station wagon to his, with as few words as possible, and I was off.

Off to 'where' was my first problem. In my haste to leave I had neglected to even determine which way I should turn out of the marina driveway. Instinct told me to head back toward the liquor store, which was to the left, and happily, not more than a mile down the road a Chevron Gas Station appeared. Could the attendant tell me how to get to Sear's in West Palm? Of course not! But he *could* tell me how to get on Interstate 95 and head in the direction of West Palm, which I did. Through interviewing a series of other innocent gas station attendants along the way I finally found the hallowed halls of the Sears Repair Shop before noon.

Contrary to my usual overly optimistic, "don't worry about it, everything will somehow be all right" attitude, a Presbyterian pessimism formed the basis for my anticipated results of the next critical minutes. I left the engine in the car, went inside the shop to check the lay of the land, noticed the repair shop to the left of the door as I entered and moved up to the front counter. I casually asked the salesperson for the manager's name, got it, and returned to the car. In five minutes, our engine and I were next in line.. The next few minutes would tell the story. It was like waiting for final exam grades and I could feel the stress. When my turn came I stood before a 250 pound, 5'8" black woman wearing blue jeans and a red stripped T-shirt with a pack of Marlboro's rolled up in one sleeve. She had biceps the size of Arnold Schwarzenegger's, her hair tied up in a white polka-dot bandana and one eye half closed to avoid the smoke from her cigarette.

"Wut cha wantz?" she challenged. She must have missed the Customer Service course.

This was not going to be easy. No chance for an impassioned speech here. So, the facts were given and my repair request made. She looked at the engine resting on the floor, came around from behind the counter and with one hand blithely lifted the engine onto the countertop. I casually stole a glance at my pitiful excuse for a muscular arm after this display of raw power and waited another ten seconds for the verdict.

"Sure, hon. We can fix this here enjin. Cost yuh $50 plus parts."

"Great! I'm, I... uh, well, my friend and I are kinda in a hurry. How soon do you think I can get her back?"

"Three weeks... if wee goz da parts".

Half-off Sail

I am not sure if I got up off the floor under my own power, but I was standing through the next part of the conversation. A second more to reorient myself, and I was asking her if she could wait just a minute. Ignoring the 'if-looks-could-kill' syndrome, I slipped past the crowd in the front part of the store and into the office area behind the counters.

"May I see Mr. Orland, please?" I said in my nicest Bob Fuller voice. To my relief, the manager appeared a moment later. The instant he saw me, his expression changed ever so slightly and, after looking me up and down, never moving his head, he cautiously asked what he could do for me.

I looked down to see if my zipper was open, which might account for the strange once-over. It was then that I realized I had not exactly dressed for the occasion. I was sporting a three-day-unwashed faded blue shirt, torn cut-off jeans, deck shoes, uncombed hair and a wild, desperate look in my eyes which would have set even me on edge. Mr. Orland quickly recovered and again asked what he could do for me. I remained self-conscious and proceeded to mutter something about nearly being killed at sea, six weeks of vacation lost, a sick friend, a $10,000 investment down the drain—all resulting from a broken Sear's engine and a projected three-week repair time.

Without responding, he walked the thirty odd feet to the repair shop entrance with me in tow, sighted our wreck among the broken lawn mowers, weed-eaters and hand tools and took a long look at the propeller before saying, "Boy, you sure did a job on this one."

I expected the next sentence to be something along the lines of, "and what the hell were you doing out in the Atlantic with a motor designed for fresh water lakes?" But instead, I got the encouraging news that with a real push he might be able to have her fixed in four days.... if they had the right parts. After twice mentioning that he had never seen anything like it, he drew me aside and spoke in a low tone.

"Look, this is a pretty new engine. Why don't you go over to the main Sear's store and see Mr. Malinowski. Sear's is pretty good about making good. I'll keep the engine here. Have him give me a call. I'll tell him that the old engine is with me and that we can't fix it. See if he'll give you a new one. Now, I can't promise anything but give it a try. At the very worst, come back and we'll try and fix this for you as soon as possible."

With sincere thanks and a bursting heart, I shook his hand and sped out to the Ford wagon. Within five minutes, I was pulling into the huge Sear's parking lot and asking questions that would guide me to Mr. Malinowski's office. My disheveled appearance made me stand out like a welfare recipient buying clothes at Macy's. Fashionable West Palm Beach assuredly had other locations for those in my attire. To make a very minor correction in my get up, I swung past the men's' shop, splashed some cologne on my face and headed for the "executive office" area.

Mr. Malinowski came out to greet me, no doubt curious after his secretary's description. Without even introducing himself, he asked me to explain again what happened. Once again, in my nicest Bob Fuller voice, I repeated the story of near death, lost vacation, sick friend, the $10,000, etc. Without a question, he retired to his office and I sat down, waiting to see if I had won the United Nations award for negotiation or a police visit. Five minutes passed, then ten and fifteen and seventeen... and he returned.

"I called Mr. Orland. He does have your engine and repairs seem unlikely. Take this receipt and go to the customer pick-up area. They'll give you a new engine. Oh, and one more thing. Don't try that stupid stunt again. The ocean is for big engines and those who know what they're doing." He turned and walked back into his office. I rose two feet off the ground and jetted down to the customer pick-up area, apologizing over my shoulder to the people I either bumped or knocked down. With a touch more confidence than in my first three encounters, I handed the receipt to the blue uniformed employee and held my breath.

"I'm not sure if I have any more of these little mother's left," he said. "Wait here a sec."

Looking over the hunting knife collection for a possible suicide instrument seemed like an appropriate place to wait out the answer. In five minutes he was back....with the engine!

"Sign here," he said, thrusting a clipboard under my nose.

I was so high I would have signed anything. With a quick scrawl I completed the only remaining task between me and success.

Hoping not to encounter a reconsidering Mr. Malinowski, I grabbed a nearby hand truck and whisked the new motor to the car. I left the parking lot as fast as six cylinders would take me. I was in touch with reality just enough to remember that Dave had no idea what was going on so the phone booth at the Texaco station down the road was my one and only stop.

"Dave? Bob," I said when he finally got to the office phone.

"Yeah, yeah I know... I thought you'd call an hour ago. I've been going nuts. So what happened?" May God forgive me for the agony I put him through, describing every detail for the next five minutes: the trip down, the lady at the repair shop, getting the manager involved, driving to the Sears's main store, the cologne, meeting Mr. Malinowski and finally, but not too quickly, the fact that there was a new engine in the back of the station wagon and that he should get ready for her.

"You dirty rat! You lousy son-of-a-bitch! I don't know whether to kiss you or kick you for putting me through all this. I can't believe it. You got a new engine!" Tears were pouring down my face I was laughing so hard. Talk about a day of mixed emotions. The tension of the morning all came out and to say that I was giddy would have been putting it mildly.

"Get the Nereus ready. I'll be back in forty-five minutes."

Somehow, there was the unspoken understanding that we were going to try it again. Although the real decision was several days away, Dave and I both knew we were going out to sea again. Not even twenty-four hours had elapsed since our heart-stopping survival course yesterday and we were ready to try again. Had we learned nothing or is human memory too short to recall pain and terror?

I was back by 1:45 p.m. Dave rushed up to greet me. When I saw him running up the dock, I got into a boxing stance not sure whether he was going to hit me or hug me. It turned out to be a hug. He was ready, the boat was ready, a beer was ready and between swigs, the Sear's story was told again.

Mounting the new engine proved problematic. For some reason, although the engine was the exact same model, it didn't quite fit the engine bracket on the stern. But, again, Rick provided some helpful suggestions, and finally, Engine #II settled into place ready to begin her work. By 2:45 p.m., we had expressed our thanks and good-byes. I fired up the engine with only five pulls on the starter cord and let her idle for a good fifteen minutes before gently moving the gearshift lever into forward. I nursed the Nereus away from the beautiful marina of St. Lucie's and into the Inland Waterway at turtle-break-in speed. Several boats zipped past, giving us those "why did they bother to come out" looks. But that was the least of our concerns. We were underway and enjoying the lush scenic view of the most picturesque canal either of us had ever seen.

The Inland Waterway is one of the most beautiful, protected boating areas in America. The tranquil watery highway hosts thousands of boats, mostly power. But the waterway offers more than just maritime activity; it also sports some of the world's most fabulous homes and is lined with extravagant tropical vegetation, every aquatic bird imaginable and wide varieties of fish seen just below the surface. One could easily cruise this paradise for a complete vacation. For us, it was simply an easy way back to the starting line, but its beauty and serenity were not lost to us.

The canals were built in the 1930's, by the Army Corp of Engineers. For this stretch of the waterway, some 72 bridges were built crossing the canal, providing vehicle access to the ocean side. A word about bridges is important. It was our first encounter with the rules of the road, so to speak: drawbridge raising. One is required to give three blasts of the horn about ½ mile from the bridge. The attendant then courteously halts the road traffic by lowering a gate, and then raises the bridge. Normally, this is accomplished with ease. But there seems to be a sport amongst most bridge attendants to see how close a boat can come to their bridge without hitting it. A game of chicken was continually played out to our teeth-chattering annoyance. One attendant won. We approached "his" bridge and found to our horror that nothing was happening after our three blasts on the horn. We turned sharply about 50 feet from the steel trap and cursed loudly to the smiling civil servant as we passed under the second time around. But, by in large, our passage was easy and a real pleasure compared to our days on the ocean.

We motored about 12 miles the first afternoon. At 5:30 p.m. or so, we found a wide part in the canal and threw out the anchor. It couldn't have been more peaceful. A lazy evening followed with gin and tonics, a modest dinner and a fabulous sunset. We felt like we were really living and doing the thing we came to do; enjoy ourselves. The next day was all motoring. Past West Palm Beach, where a moment of silent prayer was held for the managers of Sears, on through Lake Worth, past Boynton Beach, Del Ray Beach and on to our anchorage for the second night in Lake Boca Raton. It would have been great to go ashore and see what was in that lovely pink hotel, but a relaxing evening on the boat was enough. We did learn something, though. Our mast is 34½ feet high. Back at Lake Worth we passed under the Bascule Bridge, which does not open, and thought for sure we were not going to clear it. The aerial couldn't have been more than a couple of inches beneath the span as we motored through with white knuckles. It turned out that the bridge was 35 feet high.

From Lake Boca Raton, it was half a day to Hillsboro and by 2 p.m. we were back in our old slip. Pax's wasn't hard to find. Old Pax was in the bar trying to seduce the barmaid, in close to an alcoholic stupor. He was, however, sober enough to listen to our story and had the gall to laugh most of the way through. For him, nothing was traumatic. Why, compared to his days in Burma and the CIA, everything was a picnic.

The story of our misadventure circulated quickly and nautical armchair advice was liberally bestowed upon us. There were those who were amazed that we had survived in our little Venture "day sailor" boat, and that was, of course, cause for another round of beer.

But good as it was to be back and good as it was to see old friends,' Dave and I were committed to a second crossing. Time was growing short—and we were anxious to be underway.

THE SECOND CROSSING

One day of repair was all that was necessary to bring Nereus around to fighting trim. Dave and I were in lousy shape—but the boat was not bad for the punishment we had inflicted on her. Our plan was to get into a position at Hillsboro Inlet so that an early departure would be possible the next morning. Dave paid the bill. I thanked the Dockmaster for his help and advice. We showered and made one phone call-to Peter Raymond. To tell anyone else, who loved us, that we had nearly been killed at sea but were setting sail the next morning to attempt to do it again would have been somewhere in the neighborhood of sadistic. Only Peter was to know our situation. He alone would manage the information flow in such a way as to avoid a general air/sea rescue alert. Peter, of course, handled the call with his usual aplomb.

"You're where? You're what? You're crazy!"

By six o'clock we dropped the dock lines at the Sands Hotel Marina, motored under the first drawbridge, gave a quick glance toward the public dock to check the car (which we couldn't see from the water) and brought ourselves into position to wait the obligatory 15 minutes for the Hillsboro Inlet drawbridge to come up. It came up only five minutes later and, holding our breath, we pushed our new engine to full throttle in an effort to get through the strong, incoming tide.

"I hope the engine doesn't even sneeze," said Dave with some anxiety. "If we lose power, we'll be swept right into the bridge pilings."

"I know!" I called back. "She's not exactly a Percheron." One mistake here and the 7½ horsepower engine would be of minimal use—but, slowly and steadily, she pushed us through and into the open sea.

"All right!" Dave sang out. He jumped up to the bow and began looking for a likely anchorage to tie up for the night. Right behind the jetty was ideal and, with the depth sounder flickering away, indicating 20 feet beneath our keel, I brought the Nereus into the quiet lagoon. We were not sure of the anchorage, so we tied up along the wood pier, making sure we had adequate protection the length of the boat. The tide would rise further and fall again during the night. Lines were secured accordingly. With a large dinner, a few drinks, long discussions on our best strategies and much tension, we called it a night.

We wanted to be up by 4:00 a.m. to give us the full day to sail. No more night sailing for us. Lights were out by 10:30 p.m. and we each, in our own way, had to convince our very agitated brain to shut off. I'm not sure mine ever did.

"Bob, are you awake?" came Dave's soft call from the cabin.

"Yeah." I blinked.

"It's 3:30 and I can't sleep any more. Let's get a move on."

With that little encouragement I was up; I hadn't slept much anyway. We threw on some coffee and made a quick breakfast. Dave boiled his contacts while I prepared the engine. We were nearly ready and very apprehensive.

"Hey, Dave…look!" My call brought him promptly on deck. "That's the third boat I've seen and they look like they are setting a course for West End. Try and get them on the radio."

Dave raced below and started flipping toggle switches and turning dials while I held the binoculars on each ship, trying to garner more information.

"I got one!" came the excited call from below.

As Dave chattered away, I watched the parade of masts motoring slowly past. We each shared the same unspoken thought: crossing the Gulf Stream is tough enough but, with company, so many problems would be solved.

"Get under way," Dave commanded as he scrambled on deck. A flurry of activity followed; lines were released and stowed, the engine nursed to life, anchor hoisted and lashed down, sails hastily run up, equipment lashed down, navigation lights lit, charts pulled out—all within minutes.

"So, who are these guys?" I asked in a moment of calm, having motored into position behind the tenth boat.

"They're smuggling drugs to downtown Washington, so I asked if we could tag along." With a broad smile Dave gave me the good news. This was the Hillsboro Sailing Club headed for West End—all 24 boats, and we were welcome to join them. What great news! All we had to do was sail with these professionals who had hundreds of thousands of dollars in navigational equipment, lots of navigators, radios to hear our pleas for help—our own personal rescue squadron should the worst happen...again.

The apprehension vanished; the fear was gone. It was a beautiful morning with the red sky far to the east where the curtain of dawn was opening. A flight of pelicans passed to our starboard heading for the day's fishing. Things felt good. There was one small problem. There wasn't a breath of wind. Dave and I had long given up stating the obvious, so we silently motored along with the crowd, assuming the wind would pick up in an hour or so.

A brilliant sunrise broke across the sky at 5:00 a.m. and we motored. A pot of coffee was perking on the propane stove and we motored. The cabin was tidied up and we motored. And, several interesting facts began to emerge. First, a 25-foot sloop with a 7½ horsepower engine cannot motor as fast as a 36-foot sloop with a 45 horsepower engine. The higher the sun rose in the morning sky, the further behind we fell. By nine o'clock we were alone. We had taken a relative bearing on the last boat which motored merrily by. She was on a course of 078 degrees, taking the northern drift of the Gulf Stream into account.

The second fact was that with no wind we did not have enough fuel to motor 64.3 nautical miles (probably closer to 75 nautical miles with all our course corrections). At some point, and soon, we were going to have to make a decision. A decision to turn back again and hope we could make West Palm Beach. Was it possible for two dreamers to ever reach their dream? Were we s-o-o-o ill-prepared that there was no way to accomplish what we set out to do? The turning point was coming upon us. We had to make a decision soon. Either it was admit failure and turn back or go ahead and risk being engineless at sea. Another minute decided it when, literally, out of the blue, a squall approached with lightning speed. We watched it march right for us and within minutes, the sails were filled to bursting. Nereus began rocketing along. She remained hard over on her starboard side for a good half hour. In another half hour the sporadic wind died and we were once again forced to start the engine. It was now 11:45 a.m. We had been at this since 4:00 in the morning and felt certain we must be over half way there. We also had to reach a harbor by dusk since we had no spot lights powerful enough to aid our journey into an unknown anchorage in the dark. We were in a difficult position…again.

Any self-respecting reader would adamantly assure anyone willing to listen they wouldn't be in this position in the first place. We wished to god we weren't either. But, without much chatter, Dave and I knew we had few inspiring options. So, we stayed on our West End heading.

By 3:00 p.m. Dave settled down with the RDF and came out after some time to announce that we were, surprisingly enough, in great shape.

"If I can believe this reading, we are something like ten miles off of West End!"

"Ten miles, that's great, and it's only 3:00 p.m. If we can hold this slight wind and keep the engine…

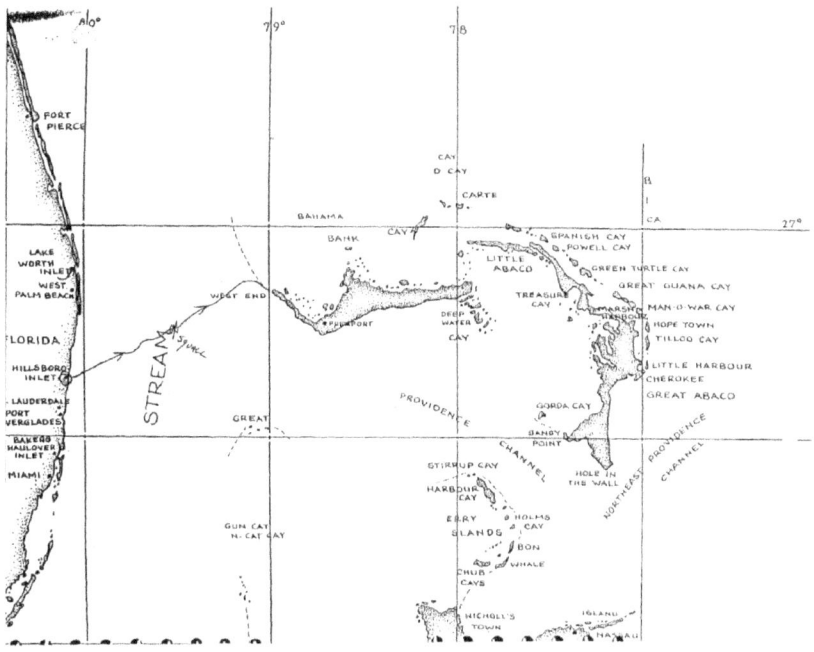

Dave grabbed my mouth! Whispering in my ear, he asked me not to even think about that engine and to please not give it any ideas. I nodded indicating yes that I understood and agreed with him completely before he took his hand away. We remained silent, looking hopefully down at the chart.

The time passed, and then at 4:15 p.m., Dave called out, "Land Ho!" The checkered tower at West End was visible four miles off on the horizon. We were a bit north of the island, thanks undoubtedly to the Gulf Stream, but we were going to make it!

By 6:00 p.m. I was asking our new heroic partner, ol' number 2, to work hard for just a few more minutes as we pushed through the swift current coming out of the beautiful harbor. We could see the bottom of the ocean floor through the crystal clear water. There was a cove with several boats at anchor so I headed toward that inviting scene. Dave readied the anchor, we scrabbled around to lower the sails, tied everything off and with the engine at idle, motored close to the shore, looking for a home. There was a hotel just ahead. With nerves slightly on edge and no knowledge of the depth of the numerous rocks below, our very cautious push forward continued. Dave was on the bow giving silent hand signals, gesturing a little left or right. I basically followed them but caught a glimpse of what I thought looked like a good spot. Ignoring Dave's call to turn left, I turned right and called for the anchor to be dropped. Dave did so, the hook caught and I killed the engine. We were stopped and safe. We had made it. No sooner had I pulled my arm back into the boat from motor maintenance than Dave came storming back.

"You didn't follow my direction! You want me on the bow guiding you in and then ignore what I think! This has to stop. If you want my guidance, take it!"

After all the hours of tension, we were at the classic moment in sailing: The tension of the crew rises in direct proportion to the closeness of the anchorage. With a short apology and a promise to never do that again, the tension quickly passed and we reset the stage. We had actually, finally, reached the Bahamas! Our trip was now ready to begin. There were drinks all around as we toasted our boat, our engine and even ourselves until late into the evening.

WESTEND AND BEYOND

The brilliant dawn brought us both on the deck by 6:30. As usual, Dave, who always slept either in the main cabin or on the deck, had a pot of water boiling. He would first boil his contact lens case for 20 minutes and then pour the water into mugs for our coffee-cocoa morning blend. There is nothing quite as pleasant as enjoying a steaming hot chocolate or a mug of coffee on deck to watch the sun rise across the crystal clear, flat, slightly green water.

The bottom was 20 feet down, and we were absolutely entranced by the clarity of the world below, open to us for the first time. I settled back against a large pillow propped up by the cabin wall and drank in the surroundings. What a peaceful morning. Even the normal chatter and banging of the cable stays in the gentle breeze seemed to add serenity to the moment.

There were some 30 boats anchored in front of the big hotel. The tide was slack and they all seemed to drift aimlessly until challenged by their anchor lines.

"Hey, look over there," Dave pointed. "That guy must have come in at night. Why would he anchor so close to the beach with a tide like this one, I wonder." Following Dave's gaze, I saw a 40-foot yacht resting in the sand on her port side almost completely out of the water.

"Christ! If the big boys make mistakes like that, I wonder what's in store for us?" Dave murmured. He went below to whip up some breakfast. By 8:15 a.m. we had the anchor on board and were gently motoring to the gas dock. The marina was cut into the island, sheltered by a long jetty. It harbored most of the power boats and had several dry docks for repairs. Gas was $2 per gallon!! An astronomical sum compared to our hometown price of 39 cents a gallon. Dave unscrewed the gas tank cap and found that we only had about a pint of fuel left. A pint! We had emptied all those jerry cans of gas into our main tank and a pint was all we had left.

"We just made it yesterday," he said, almost reverently. As he topped the six-gallon tank, I meandered around the dock, trying to strike up a conversation....any conversation would do. We needed information about what was out there, the best places to go, the tides—everything. If it was not abundantly clear from all that preceded our arrival, we really did not have a clue what we were doing. What got us here was perseverance and divine intervention. The fact that we did survive *implied* there was some degree of competence mixed into this miracle. Luck seemed a more likely explanation. So, the big question on our minds that first morning was, would our luck hold as we headed out to a New World? From our new perspective, statues to Columbus' courage were not nearly tall enough.

By 10:00 a.m. the customs office was open and we registered. Dave took down the yellow quarantine flag and replaced it with the black, yellow and red flag of the Bahamas. We had expected the boat to be searched for drugs or guns, but they did not so much as even look at our yacht. She must have been too small to see from the Customs House. We paid the Dockmaster a few bucks to tie up for the day, gave the battery to the repair shop for recharging and set off to explore the island.

Our first stop was the hotel. It was a pleasant hotel and to us, it looked like the St. Regis. A quick scan of the lobby told us there were no available young ladies anxious for our company so we headed over to the local supermarket where the prices limited what we loaded into the check-out basket. By 1:00 p.m., we were back on the boat, ready for lunch. We ate leisurely and just soaked up the tropical surroundings. The harbor had moderate to light boat traffic. The sky was filled with high puffy white clouds. The breeze was ever so light. The squawk of seagulls and terns filled in the silence. And it felt good just to be lazy. We tried to talk with fellow yachters but by 3:00 p.m. we had gained nothing from the local captains in terms of nautical intel, so we recovered our battery and decided to motor back out to "our" spot.

With the anchor set, we spent an hour swimming around the boat in the clear, warm water. Although there was not much below worth seeing, we could not help but spend all of our time just swimming and diving.

We were back on deck by 5:00 p.m., put the tape deck into action and mixed warm gin and tonics. We had not settled in for more than five minutes when a dinghy pulled up alongside, rowed by a man in his mid-thirties with a good tan, unkempt hair and three days growth of beard.

"May I come aboard, Skipper?" he said slightly out of breath. We were only too eager for company and immediately had him in the cockpit with a drink in his hand.

"My name is Ed. Ed Hanson. My wife and three kids are over there on the 28-foot *O-Day*." His wife waved as we looked.

"My brother and his son are in the small yellow boat behind us. We're from Minnesota, he's from Texas. Where are you fellas from?" Out popped our story and within half an hour we had been invited for supper on their boat. Ed's invitation to dinner was viewed as a good sign our story did not scare him as much as it scared us in the telling. We quickly readied the dinghy and followed him over to Hanson's On the Sea Restaurant.

The Hanson's were one of those "nice" families; they looked nice, talked nice and had a warm, casual attitude that made us feel more than welcome. He, as it turned out, was a minister. And they were doing almost exactly what Dave and I were doing only with a slightly bigger boat, which they had trailed from their home in Minnesota to Fort Lauderdale. Stories were shared while we were munching an excellent batch of conch fritters. "So, what's your destination?" Dave finally asked.

"Well, it's hard to say. We're basically trying to sail around the Abaco's (the island chain to our immediate east) but the wind and currents really tell us where we'll go."

It was only too true. You may want to sail to St. Thomas, but the wind and current will dictate (if even possible) the course length of time it will take. The "sea conditions" may change your destination. We were beginning to understand this basic law of the sea only too well. Understanding centered on the word "acceptance" of what nature presents.

Ed continued, "We want to set out tomorrow for Mangrove Cay...." And, before he could finish, I was asking if we could join their little fleet. Mangrove Cay was some 15 miles northeast and looked like a nondescript uninhabited blob with no sheltering harbor on the chart.

"Well, sure. The more the merrier."

"Boy, you aren't kidding," chuckled Dave.

A plan (unusual in these waters, it seemed) began to take shape as we talked on. We had really wanted to stay in this nice, safe harbor longer, but getting out to sea again was necessary if we were ever to make a voyage out of this adventure. With our general directions set, we said our good nights, rowed back to our boat and sat down silently to enjoy some music until about 8:00 p.m.

"I'm not really ready to call it a night. Let's go ashore and see if there's any action," Dave said, breaking my reverie.

"Uh.....sure."

Within ten minutes we were dressed in our Sunday finest and ready to board our small water taxi. By the time we landed our two-man rubber inflatable on the beach our pants were wet in the seat and one of us had worked up a fine sweat rowing *us* in. The rubber "duck" was pulled high off the beach and tied to a near-by shed. We puffed up our 6'1" bodies as large as possible and walked into the hotel lobby, just waiting for the onslaught of beautiful women ready to spend the night with two good looking guys.

An hour later we were still waiting. There were simply no unattached beauties strolling around. Finally, after cruising back and forth between the lobby and the bar, we spotted some.

"Mine looks pretty good," Dave said with a wink "but yours is ugly."

Trying to grab him, before I was stuck with Miss Piggy, ended with us in front of our quarry at the same time. Then, with all the cool tact that comes from years of training (gleaned from the *How NOT to Pick-up Girls* technique), we began.

"Hi. I'm Dave and this is Bob."

A long pause was followed by weak "Hi."

"Uh, we were just about to take a walk outside around the pool. Would you like to join us?"

"No."

I missed the hint of doubt in that "no", the hint that invites you to press your case. A very nervous smile crossed our lips. "Well, it's been real nice talk'n to you ladies. Maybe we'll see you tomorrow."

Our dreams shattered, we took our bruised egos back to the dinghy and rowed home, a real fine evening for our second night. And this was the best hotel in the Bahamas. One could only imagine our prospects for companionship on uninhabited cays along the way.

At dawn we set sail against the incoming tide. Unlike **all** our other departures this one was greeted with excitement and anticipation. Our friends provided a sense of safety—and we were sailing to cays or islands (pronounced "keys") with an overall water depth of 10 - 20 feet en route. This little fact gives the novice sailor a remarkable security blanket. For one thing, you can see the bottom and have at least a sense of the speed and direction your boat is headed. This may, of course, bear no relation to the direction you wish to go, but, for us, it was a luxurious perspective.

The other benefit we now had was that at any point we could "stop-the-action" and put on the brakes. Throwing the anchor overboard has a remarkably powerful way of preventing any forward progress and, with the anchor out, the sails down, the top zipped up all around, two very courageous New Jersey boys could cower in the cabin without making sailing fools of themselves in a serious squall.

We rounded Indian Cay, a rock no bigger than our boat just half a mile north of the main island, and set our course for 90 degrees due east, aiming for the little speck on the chart called Mangrove Cay. The wind was blowing from a perfect direction, directly behinds us, so we put Nereus wing on wing for several hours. Wing on wing is positioning the sails on opposite sides of each other, which spreads canvas everywhere. It is cause for some tricky sailing because the captain must keep the wind directly behind the boat in order to keep both sails filled. By 9:30 a.m. we were beginning to head off course and put our sails to starboard. The wind was not overly strong, so we enjoyed a relatively easy sail. In fact, it seemed just short of paradise: mild winds, warm sun, clear skies, and the visible bottom slipping away beneath us. With all these good things happening, it was hard to remember what all the panic was about just the other day.

About noon, Ed called over the radio, "We're stopping for lunch and a swim. Do you want to join us?"

Dave looked at me as if to say, "Is he kidding? Of course!" Our little fleet came together and for several minutes, drifted over the bottom. Dave and I followed, but after a while began to wonder aloud why we were just drifting.

"Uh, Ed. Why don't we anchor?" I finally called over.

"We're looking for a rock."

"A rock?"

"Yeah. You find fish under the rocks, so if we can locate a rock we'll have a great lunch."

And, sure enough, in time he found a rock that brought out the anchors. Over the side went Ed's brother, a man we had not even met yet, and, we learned—a man with no fear. We set our anchor and enjoyed a swim before lunch while beginning to learn about diving. As they expected, brother John soon came up with a grouper and they—not we—had a good lunch.

"I think we'd better learn that trick," said Dave taking another bite of his peanut butter and mayonnaise sandwich.

"Yep, sure does look tastier than what we're eating."

Refreshed, we pulled up anchors an hour later and set out again. By 4:30 p.m. we were about to anchor around Mangrove Cay and, by a lucky fluke, we picked the northern tip of the small, round, unsheltered island as our spot. Most yachters were packed in at the northwest and western shore. The rest were scattered in an unorganized fashion beyond the point.

Dave threw out the anchor as we maneuvered into position and then, stripping off his two-week, unwashed, yellow, sweat-stained "I Ran the New York Marathon 1977" T-shirt, dove in and spent several minutes *planting* the old Danforth anchor on the rocky bottom to make sure we would not be dragged off our unprotected spot should the wind come up in the night.

What a paradise Mangrove Cay was—solidly covered with the trees the Cay was named for, bordered by natural sugar-colored, sandy beaches, surrounded by clear water with a momentary backdrop of orange paint all over the western sky from the setting sun. Drinks were rustled up as the other boats drew alongside our position, forming an informal connection of cockpits, called rafting, we learned, allowing people to bounce from boat to boat while everyone benefited from a cassette tape of sea songs Dave Powell, my old buddy, had provided me as a "good-luck, you stupid fool" departure gift. Beef stew with mixed veggies sprayed with pasteurized Kraft American cheese in a pressurized can (one of our favorites) was a welcome dinner. It was followed by a surprise glass of cognac from Ed's private cache to cap off a perfect day. With glasses drained, goodnights were shared and lines released, the Hanson boats drifted some 20 yards astern to set their anchors. It sure was a peaceful night. The peace seemed like it would last forever.

At 2:00 a.m., the peaceful night was interrupted by the distinctive banging of the halyards against the mast signaled a rapid rise in the wind. Within minutes Dave was hurling blankets and cushions into the cabin from his starlight bunk topside and pounding on the bulkhead.

"Bob!" That was all he needed to say. I was getting good at bolting up through the forward hatch in no time flat, ready for action. By instinct, the first thing I did was check the bow anchor line (yes, it was still there) and look at the shore to see if we were moving. We were bouncing but did not appear to be drifting.

"Ok, up here!" I called back from the now wildly bucking foredeck.

"Stow everything!" he shouted.

I raced aft, almost diving into the cockpit, as waves started violently slapping at the hull. Chaos had seemingly come out of nowhere. The last thing I remembered was we were having a peaceful night.

"Bob, watch the dinghy!"

With that, I whipped around to face the stern just in time to see the wind neatly untie our raft and launch it across the waves. It literally danced across the top of the waves headed for Mozambique, I was sure. But there was no time to watch our olive drab/orange lifeboat race off into the night. With things more or lease secure on deck, we moved inside and stood in the cabin with arms outstretched holding down the canvas cabin hood. The wind velocity jumped dramatically. We could see search lights from boats to the west waving wildly back and forth. The sea was in a foaming broil and the Nereus was bucking in the shallow surf like a western stallion.

"Man, this sure is someth'n. I've never seen anything like it. I remember once in Colorado watching…, no, it was Kansas. I was watching this twister come across the field and, man, I'd really like to have a drink. How ya do'n?"

"Fine," I said in a flat voice that would inform anyone that I was very uptight. Dave rattled on and on and on. I said nothing.

"What's the matter?" he asked.

"Noth'n."

"Well, something must be bugging you. Why so quiet?"

"Uh."

"Come on, talk to me."

"Ok! Well, let me put that more calmly… ok. . ." Then, laughing, I made an observation. "You know that course in communications we taught?"

"Yeah."

"Well, we're not doing such a good job communicating, are we?"

"No, but… what's up?"

"Well, it seems like you talk a blue streak in tough situations, and I keep it all inside…" and we began talking in the cabin of our bucking boat about how Dave manages fear through chatter and I through silence. It was agreed, on the spot, that Dave would talk less and I would talk more. One would think, by now, our individual styles, our idiosyncrasies, would be well known to each other. But, here we were, working out our "communication style" differences in a raging storm. And, without intending to, the conversation in the storm helped pass the time, get our mind off our frightening situation and improve our crisis management skills for the days ahead. You just never know when the time for "meaningful conversation" will present itself. Meantime, the wind was increasing. Boats we could see through blinding rain were spinning around their anchor chains like toys; their running lights tracing crazy patterns in the oil black sky.

"If one of those babies break free, it'll come right at us!" I nearly screamed, looking to our south at all the dancing boats, keenly aware we were downwind of everybody. The extended centerboard began banging on the sea floor and I was more than concerned it would come right up through the floor of the cabin if I didn't bring it up. On the other hand, if I brought it up, it would make us less stable than we were. There was no right answer, so we left it down, prayed no huge wave would crash us into the bottom and hung on. Each passing wave forced us to hold our breath, unsure if we would have a centerboard in our lap, or just a wildly pitching boat.

And, right about 3:15 a.m., the wind suddenly dropped off. The howling subsided and the sea grew increasingly calm. Dave finally made his way into the vee berth and roused Ed on the radio.

"Hey, that was somethin'! Over." Ed called back to Dave's opening.

"We didn't sign up for the advanced course in anchoring. What the hell was that all about? Over."

"That was one of the quickest, worst winds I've ever seen. I had those winds pegged at 50 knots on my little wind gauge here. Have you seen John? Over."

Dave and I looked around and could see nothing. A brief search from several other boats, whose chatter now filled the airways, brought no news and with some trepidation, we signed off, hoping for the best.

By dawn a scene unfolded that took our breath away. Five huge yachts were aground on the west side of the cay. By chance they had been anchored directly in the path of the storm. Again, more experienced yachtsmen were having trouble and—by luck—we had missed near disaster. We had lost our rubber dingy and were in the curious predicament of now having no way to rescue ourselves should our stout little ship sink. Thoughts of sinking seemed to be a reoccurring theme. Still, we had improved our pattern of communication, the assumption being that we would now be able to sink with verbal clarity.

The other interesting occurrence was that even after Dave had planted the anchor in what turned out to be hard, almost volcanic sand the night before, we had dragged some 50 feet. It was not John that had disappeared in the night... it was us!

With our nerves slightly realigned by breakfast, we rallied around Ed's boat and spent a good half hour reviewing the storm. The most indifferent one of us all was John, who was in a 21-foot wreck of a boat with his 9-year-old son. It was my impression that he should have the most to fear from the night time of chaos, yet he expressed the least concern. I promptly concluded the man had a serious psychological disorder. Of course, anyone watching what we were doing would no doubt mutter something about "glass houses" before hearing further pronouncements on the psychological soundness of other.

Near lunch time, this "glass house" issue was to be played out in full in a way only Woody Allen could have dreamed up. The pre-lunch sail had been excellent. We were moving along at some 5 knots all morning, and, of course, if you can image that. By 11:00 a.m. we were about one mile north of the Hanson's two boats—not by design but because the Nereus could not point as close into the wind as could they. We were headed for the next cay and the well protected harbor of Great Sale Cay. The 20-knot wind was coming directly from the southern tip of the lone island so we were sailing as best we could and making great time—somewhat north of our destination. In retrospect, we realized we should have tacked a mile earlier, which would have brought us closer to our target. But America's Cup racing boats make errors in tacking decisions, so we, like them, sail and learn. It seemed to sum up our whole experience thus far. What else could we possibly learn?

By noon, arrangements were made over the radio to anchor at what was guessed to be about two miles off the coast. Ed's family was already anchored by the time we sailed in behind them. I had the tiller and was digging out the stern anchor while Dave went forward to prepare the bow anchor. The plan was to come up behind the Hanson's and, some 40 feet away, drop the sails and throw out the stern anchor, to bringing us gently alongside. I set the fenders out along the starboard side to cushion our union. All was ready. I had laid the coiled stern anchor line on the deck with the small 15-pound Danforth on top and unattached to the steer cleat.

I was intently focused on steering us close to the Hanson's boat, without hitting it when I called, "Dave, come back and give me a hand. I can't work the tiller, sails *and* throw out the anchor."

Dave came back and, at what he judged to be the right moment, released the main sail sheet and then threw out the stern anchor. He casually watched the anchor line to see how much was left before cleating it off. We were almost perfectly alongside when....PLOP!!

Aghast, Dave turned with complete disbelief in his voice and ever so positively, said, "You stupid, freaking idiot! You forgot to tie off the line!"

Half-off Sail

"You mean you just threw the anchor overboard?" I bridled at his attack. Worse yet, was the realization that he was absolutely right.

"Yes, I threw it overboard, but you were supposed to tie it off!"

"I thought *you* would tie it off when you figured out how much line was needed."

"You should always tie off the line! How was I....watch out!! We're going to hit the Hansons!"

I swung the tiller away and with the sails luffing the boat just stalled. The current started carrying us away from our intended lunch stop.

"Dave, throw out the bow anchor! I'm going in after our other one." Without waiting for written approval of this suggestion, I dove into the water and swam out to where I thought the anchor might be. I took a breath, looked under water for a minute and spotted the line. I pulled my head out of the water, gulp down some air, prepared for a 20-foot dive to bring up the anchor, and turned to tell Dave I'd found it.

A shiver went down my submerged body. There was the Nereus drifting further and further away with Dave hanging off the bow pulpit, thigh deep in the water and thrashing about like a fish on a line.

Why was Dave hanging off the side of the boat? He surely didn't think he was going to touch bottom. I pondered this bizarre scene for another second and dove for the anchor that was rapidly receding from view as I drifted in the current. Again, I gulped in a lung full of air, dove and blew gently out, equalizing the pressure slowly all the way down. The bottom was pure white sand with short sea grass dotting the rolling contour. I grabbed the anchor and with a heave-ho, brought it to the surface. Gasping for air and treading water furiously, I looked around for Dave. He was back on the boat, cursing a blue streak and, from what I could make out, trying to start the engine.

"Hey! Come pick me up!" I called. I watched and knew that Dave would never be able to start the engine. I hardly knew what magical things I did to get the fool thing started half the time. This could be a long wait. Rather than wait, I began swimming toward the boat with the anchor in one hand. After three exhausting minutes, I looked up to find the boat had drifted further away! Dave was almost beside himself with rage, and I was wondering how long I could swim carrying a 15-pound anchor.

Meanwhile, the Hansons had settled down for a nice quiet lunch with the live Bob & Dave Show for some of the best seaside entertainment in the Bahamas.

Back to ringside. "Dave! I can't do this too much longer!"

"So, what do you want me to do that I'm not doing?" he screamed. "If you had tied off that line we wouldn't be in this mess!" Just when you think you know somebody, this sort of thing happens. I could see the boat. What I saw was a tower of rage. After what must have been 50 pulls on the starter cord, he was unable to get the engine going and finally, giving up, went forward to set the bow anchor. This time he succeeded and quickly dove in to help me. I was shot. He, on the other hand, was so angry he had enough energy to rescue me, the anchor and a small basketball team. Together we nursed the lifeless hunk of steel forward and finally alongside the boat. We rested, just hanging on to the fender, now serving as lifesaving equipment instead of a boat protection, courtesy for the Hansons. The beautifully crafted side ladder was still stowed so hoisting ourselves back onto the boat took an exhausting combination of pushing and pulling each other up and over the side. Once onboard we lay in the cockpit for several minutes wheezing and gasping for air. Finally, Dave laughed. "Hungry?"

"I think the Hansons are done eating by now, and the show is over. Shall we just go on?" Some lunch break.

"By the way, why were you hanging over the bow railing?" Dave's eyes rolled back into his head as he told me the story. "When I saw you dive in I went forward to throw out the bow anchor. I still can't believe it but I slipped and fell overboard, myself. I guess what you saw was me hanging on for dear life. I was so pissed hanging there that, after a second, I literally threw myself back into the boat. Then I went back to start that stupid engine. You were getting too far away and I wanted to motor over and pick you up—needless to say the engine wouldn't start. I was so pissed. Then you kept yelling at to me to stop the boat. God! What did ya think I was doing up here!?"

"Well….I really couldn't tell….tell me the story again ," I chuckled, stuffing a cracker in my mouth. So back to the question floating in the air just before lunch; what else could we possibly learn? I had no idea how to sum up some key take away from this event.

The grand finale was only minutes away. The Hansons were ready to leave, and we had to get under way. I started the engine with two pulls (Dave nearly beat me up for that). Boy, did I know how to start engines. But, the truth was, he had warmed the thing up with all his earlier effort and with a minor carburetor adjustment it caught immediately. I then proceeded to motor right into the side of the Hanson's boat. Everyone was screaming, trying to push us off. We only bumped her slightly, but the whole affair left major psychological damage to all concerned. Can you imagine the conversation among the Hansons as we pulled away?

We motored/sailed for two hours and anchored for the night in a well-protected harbor at Sale Cay. We swam for an hour, rowed ashore in our small inflatable backup dingy, hiked along the sandy beach, trained the binoculars on an impressive flock of crane-like birds and dried off over warm gin and tonics late in the afternoon. Music and a fine dinner of chicken chow mein capped off the beautiful evening.

"So, where do you want to go next?" I asked, not really sure the conversation would lead to a meaningful conclusion. Dave rummaged under the seat cushion and pulled out a collection of charts. After pouring over each selection for several minutes, he made his decision.

"I think we should head up around Carter Cay and then down along the coast of the Abaco's, heading for Man of War. It says great things in the guidebook about the place. You know - lush, beautiful, a tropical paradise with good anchorages. Listen… then we could come around and head for Bimini," Dave folded his hands confidently on the butcher-block table and waited for my agreement.

"Naw," I finally said after a few moments of thought. Dave's "why-the-hell not" look encouraged me to explain.

"Look, I agree that Man of War is beautiful, but it would require us to sail completely against the current. If we made it, and that is a big "if", we might have a great sail to Bimini. But that looks like miles of open ocean and you know how good we are at that. I'm not sure where to go, but that's not the easiest route, to say the least."

Dave pondered this for a while and finally agreed. It was a tough decision for him because he held strong beliefs about the adventure and the beauty of some of those distant cays.

"So, what do you suggest?" he finally said.

"Don't know. It looks like we have very little choice. Maybe up to Carter and then back along some of these northern cays," I said, tracing my finger along the chart.

"Well, that's possible. It would give us more time to play and at this point, all we've done is work our fool heads off. You may have a good point."

"Yeah. Let's talk about it tomorrow," I said and climbed into my comfortable vee berth. The red glow of the cabin light was strong enough to allow an hour of reading. The book I had selected was definitely inappropriate; *The Earthquake in San Francisco,* Dave's was worse- *Jaws.*

Neither of us scrambled out of bed at dawn. With the pressure off to make time we started the day by enjoying our rest. At 10, the two Hanson's boats motored up to announce they were going ahead and would meet us somewhere along the way. We waved them good-by and, as they moved away, Dave turned to me and with a low laugh said, "Now, I wonder why they wanted to leave us?"

"Yesterday comes to mind," I said, and we both started retelling that botched anchoring story.

Half-off Sail

We were alone now, but our solo status did not seem all that troubling. We had learned a great deal in the last several days, and we were gaining confidence.

"Ok, so let's head off to Carters. Then we can work our way back." The one thing we'd learned about sailing was: you go where the sea and the wind take you.

"Right." I said with no great desire to leave but got up and slowly, like he, began to put the boat in order for departure.

The sail to Carter's was pleasant. Billowing cumulus clouds filled the sky like snow-covered mountains. As we passed along the northwestern shore off Great Sale Cay, we began verbally daydreaming about a restaurant under the water that would be the most unique dining experience ever. The water was so clear and the coral reef created stunning beauty everywhere just below the waves. We carried on with the make-believe detailed plans for an hour or more, loving every minute.

It was dusk as we approached the mouth of the Carter Cay harbor. Twenty sailboats could be seen peacefully laying at anchor. The whole setting was tranquil and inviting. The sails were down, the motor was purring and the boat was rigged for anchoring.

"How do we get into this place?" I asked.

"There's a channel near here somewhere. At least the book says there is."

"What's the depth of the rest of this area?" I asked, sweeping my hand around the open water in front of the harbor.

Dave looked up the figures and called out, "About three to four feet.

"Well, hell, let's pull up the center board and go straight in. After all, we only draw 18 inches."

Dave cranked up the centerboard. The cream colored, sandy bottom rose rapidly toward our hull as we turned in. Dave moved to the bow for a better look, even though we both knew we'd hit ground before he could spot anything that required course correction. I slowed the Nereus down to a crawl and watched Dave intensely.

"The rudder just kicked up!" I called as the lower section caught the sand. Since it extended three feet below the hull, this was no immediate concern. It just told us we were in three feet of water. Eighteen inches to go before the hull hit. The depth sounder was useless at this point, but I couldn't get forward to turn it off.

"Yeah, I heard it. Come starboard one point."

I made the slight correction and we continued on. I looked up and noticed that people were appearing on nearly all the boats in the harbor and everyone was looking our way. I looked behind us, saw nothing exceptional, and turned back to my work. I wondered what they were looking at. Dave called out several more directions and asked for another reduction in speed. At least if we hit it would be gently. His eyes swept the course in front of us, looking for an unexpected coral head. Coral heads were a real concern. They were uncharted and sat just out of view, waiting to tear the bottom out of your boat if hit. It reminded me of driving at night and hitting a loose boulder on the highway. Only someone who has done this could have that image come to mind at a time like this. The depth sounder suddenly jumped up a notch to a reading of 10 feet... then 12.. .15.. .16.

"How does it look? I think we're through."

"We're home free. Bring us into that open space between the shore and those two sloops over there," he called back in a jubilant voice.

I followed his instructions exactly, and he threw the hook out right where *he* wanted us to be.

We were safe. I looked up and found that people were cheering us from their boats. Our travel agent had not mentioned anything about a welcoming committee. Strange. Did all the harbors have such hospitality? I wondered. I could not put my finger on it but something was definitely different.

PLAY TIME IN THE SHALLOWS

The nearest boat was supporting four people along the port rail.

"Hey, when you guys settle in, come on over for a drink," called one of the onlookers.

"Great... be over in a jiffy!" Dave called back.

We made a quick effort to tidy up, pumped up the small rubberdingy—which we had never intended to use - and made our way smartly over to our new-found friends.

"Thanks for the invite," I said, scrambling over the side of their 36-foot Hinckley.

"You guys deserve it. By the way, what's your draft?" asked our host, pointing to the Nereus with one hand and shaking my outstretched hand with the other.

"I'm Bob, and this is Dave. Eighteen inches. Why?"

"Eighteen inches!" The smile almost left his face. "What sail boat draws 18 inches out here? No wonder you didn't get stuck on the sand bar—we all had bets on how far in you'd make it and the loser was going to go and tow you off! Well, I'll be... looks like nobody made any money. You guys aren't as stupid as we all thought."

I tried to assure him that we *were* as stupid as they all thought; we just had the right boat for this one occasion.

It was a friendly collection of yachting families. The haughty barriers mainland sailors have among themselves, based on yachting apparel, length of boat, color of one's sails and the polish of chrome, are dropped quickly once anchored in a remote harbor. Nevertheless, we were the smallest fish in this very big pond. All their yachts sunk their teeth into the sand between Big Carrier Cay and Gully Cay, a distance of 800 feet - a spot open to the wind from the south but shallow in all directions, preventing any wave build-up. The result of all this strategic placement was a peaceful night.

Dawn brought a flawless day streaming across the horizon. Several yachts had already continued their voyage but for us it was a day to play. There was the usual morning clean up. Why we had to constantly clean up a 25-foot sail boat was only discovered later. Apparently, on sail boats there is a magical force field that develops around all storage cabinets, forcing the doors open at night causing the stored items to reappear all over the cabin the following morning. We did not fully understand this phenomenon for several months and were forced to carry on the constant clean up amid curses and befuddlement.

By midmorning we were ready. Our goal was to sail out to just inside the northern reef. Once there, we planned to anchor a safe distance away and explore the reef and water palace below. We stopped far short of the reef after noticing an old freighter stranded on the rocks. It was ample warning, and we were content with our spot. We had crossed over a large coral labyrinth about 200 feet before the reef. It was 8-10 feet below the surface and offered some great diving for amateurs. The anchor was set, the ladder swung over the side, and with mask and fins dressing our tan bodies, we jumped over the side.

It was a wonderland. Although somewhat barren in spots, the brilliant purple sea fans waved to us from all directions. There were few fish but in as much as this was our first dive, everything looked exciting. We stayed within an 80-foot radius of the boat—out of fear of the unknown and the strong current.

Dave went nuts picking up shells, starfish and sea fans. We swam down to the underwater caverns, poking our noses everywhere in the warm, clear water, and within an hour, had so much treasure that I began to ferry a load back to the boat. It was a long swim against the current, but I was in no hurry. Dave stayed out diving for a while, having the time of his life. My leisurely surface swim back was interrupted by a frantic call from Dave, forty feet away.

"Bob! There's a huge fish coming your way!!"

I plunged my face under the water for a better look. I couldn't see anything.

"BOB!!" Dave called again. "It's coming right at you!"

I still saw nothing. I kept wondering what I was supposed to do with this information. I couldn't get out of the water, I couldn't swim any faster, and I surely couldn't talk to the challenger.

But Dave kept giving me position reports: "it's circling to your right....now it's behind you..."

I finally called back, "Dave—I can't do anything with that information. Stop scaring the shit out of me!"

Having not seen this monster, I pulled myself out of the water onto the Nereus very relieved to have reached her with everything intact. From the bow my eyes swept the water, looking for Dave's fish. I saw nothing. Dave finally came alongside, and once on the boat, retold the whole encounter. What Dave saw was probably a 1000-pound Jew fish. They are totally harmless creatures and I actually wished I had seen it. Instead, my imagination ran amuck and a 5000-pound shark was all I had pictured.

Our little (actually huge) reef guardian did not intimidate us enough to prevent us from going back into the water, and on into the late afternoon, we explored the sea gardens amid barracuda, an occasional shark and a host of more pleasant creatures. I must say, the barracuda and sharks were frightening, especially the barracuda. Their long, razor-sharp teeth with jaws partly opened looked extremely menacing as they hovered 10 feet away. We couldn't tell if they would attack or just watch us. Memories of southern California days (my boyhood home) where 6 foot barracuda reportedly attacked swimmers along the Malibu coast did not calm my nerves. We eventually gave them a wide berth and continued our explorations. By 4:00 p.m. we motored back against the tide and nestled into "our" spot 40 minutes later. Drinks around, music and stories filled the starry evening. We were enjoying ourselves.

The next day the Hansons sailed into the little harbor and we could not have been happier to see them. Later, Ed and John went off to redo our trip to the reef from the day before, and Dave and I —along with Mary, Ed's wife—made up a batch of conch fritters.

Conch is one of God's real jokes. It is one of the ugliest creatures that ever existed. And, the meat is tough. I took a hammer and pounded each piece to a pulp. Dave soaked it in lemon juice and tomato sauce for two hours and still it was like eating rubber-bands, but we appreciated the change in diet from canned stew and cheese spray. .

The island offered little to explore, but we did get ice at the weather station. Ice. What a treat in this sun-pounding environment. Through evening conversation it was decided by all the members of our reunited tribe that we would sail on the next morning toward the northwest. We departed at a civilized hour heading north through the sand bar around Old Yankee Cay and inside the reef. It was tricky going. The chart had little "+", indicating danger, all over the place. The exact location of the coral and rocks was total guesswork. At one point, Dave shouted, "Hey, something's happened to Ed!"

I looked back, but he looked fine to me. "What's wrong?" I asked.

"I don't know. I just saw the boat stand on its nose for a second and then bounce back."

"Sounds like he hit something. Try to get him on the phone."

Dave scrambled below and a minute later, had Mary on the air. They chatted awhile, and then Dave came back up to report.

"She said they hit a coral head. The kids were thrown around a bit and Ed's checking for damage. They'll call back if they need us."

We sailed in a circle (which, for us, was easy) for about half an hour and finally got a call that all was well with the Hansons. We set out again, but our little fleet was now widely scattered. Since John had no radio, he knew nothing of the event but we could still see him several miles ahead. We were headed toward Pelican Rock and a more southerly route, rather than the shallow sand bar and reef-infested waters of the northern route to Grand Cay John had favored.

We radioed what we saw back to Ed and found him obliged to follow his brother. We wished him good sailing and brought Nereus close into the wind.

It was interesting to sail up the southern side of the island chain toward Double Breasted Cay. We had to swing around several sand bars but, on occasion, we could see the Hansons sailing up the other side. By 2:00 p.m. they were lost from view. The surrounding scenery was so beautiful it hardly mattered who was along. The entire trip was done in no more than nine feet of clear water. If we had had a glass-bottomed boat, we could not have seen more. Even though the bottom was sandy and there was not much to see, the boat seemed suspended in air, supported by the transparent water.

And then the most unbelievably graceful thing happened.

"Bob, look!" I followed Dave's pointed finger and saw them.

"Wow—two porpoises!!"

"No, I don't think so," Dave said thoughtfully.

The two mammals glided in front of the bow and made a slow turn along our port beam.

"See how black they are? And, look, they're breathing. That means they're dolphins."

"Ok, they're dolphins. This is incredible! Let's get a closer look."

I swung the tiller wide to starboard and brought us around. It was a futile effort, of course, as the dolphins were long gone. But what a sight it had been. They were so close we could have touched them. We both wanted to jump in after them and play. We were euphoric and feeling as close to the sea and nature and the beautiful earth as we ever could. The dolphins—so graceful and so close. It was as if we touched something from another planet. They were only inches away—and yet, they were in another world, impossible for us to reach.

We brought the Nereus centerboard up near Double Breasted Cay. The water was shallow enough to walk waist deep on the sandy bottom. Thank God we drew less than two feet; here we would have been forced a mile to the south without that helpful design feature.

We approached the southeastern split at 4:10 p.m. I know that because we had the radio on and, fortuitously, the time was mentioned. The narrow channel was tricky, which put Dave back in his favorite position on the bow using gentle hand signals to guide our course. Once through the sand bars, we motored up the channel between two low islands: the one to port very narrow but a perfect fortress against the sea, the one to starboard was more substantial, lightly shrub-covered and supporting several sandy beaches.

Dave guided us a half-mile up the more substantial island and we dropped the hook in mid-channel. It was so protected and so picturesque that we stayed for two days without moving. Nothing of tremendous interest happened. We just sat in the sun, swam lazily around the boat, explored the island by foot, read, slept, and listened to music. We lacked cold beer and other obvious creature comforts but, all in all, this was not bad. In fact, I can't recall a more tranquil time.

Dave and I had learned to capitalize on our compatibles and utilize our differences to great effect. High among our strengths was our mutual ease to converse. Granted, we had taught a course in "Communication" at night school for Thomas Edison College, but beyond the techniques of good communication skills, we were great at rambling philosophical bullshit discussions. And it was on Double Breasted Cay that we whiled away the hours deep in conversation. It was great and one of the best parts of our long voyage.

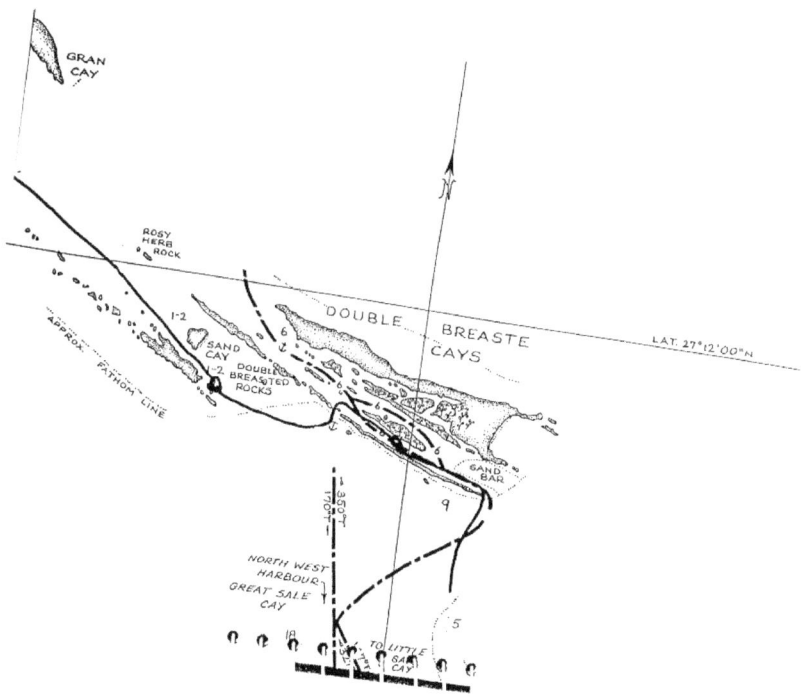

On our second day, one disruptive event did occur. As we lounged comfortably on the deck, jumping overboard to periodically cool off and having not a care in the world our private world was invaded with the arrival of another boat. On this vast body of water we now were crowed. The alien was a huge 54-foot Hatteras cabin cruiser that dropped anchor within sight of us. Disturbed by the proximity, at one point, Dave trained the binoculars on them, to see who these cretins were and noticed three girls and three guys. That wasn't unusual except Dave started reporting some very problematic observations. As the pirate flag flew high above them, their deck was littered with naked sun bathers and beer cans.

"Don't tell me anymore!" I said burying my lips into another slug of hot gin and tonic. The recent weeks of involuntary chastity meant my manhood had a hair pin trigger, and I was in no mood for Russian roulette.

"No, come on, you've got to see this."

With reluctance I took the glasses to watch for a second to placate Dave. An hour later I settled back to nap with a severe case of eye strain and a bit of envy. I suggested a swim but reached for the first aid salve when Dave hit the water and joined him later instead.

The next day things seemed a little crowded so we decided to head toward Grand Cay. With all in order, we headed out, motoring against the gentle current flowing between the parallel islands. Not long into our trip, there appeared to be a rather substantial break in the land on southern side.

Dave pointed to the break and gave a quick look at the chart. "If we can make it through that cut it will save about two miles of 1 to 2- foot shallows."

The tide was swift, and water poured through the opening so fast it was clear we would never make it back once we committed to go through. This was going to be tricky. Without much thought, I cranked up the centerboard, swung Nereus around and pointed the bow straight at the cut. Dave raced forward.

"Looks good," he called. "Take her a little more starboard… we're drifting. Harder now—bring her higher!"

I was struggling to see and it felt like trying to thread the eye of a needle with a 25-foot sailboat. One mistake and the bottom would be torn out by the coral. Another smart move by the Mensa twins!

"Let me know if we can't make it as soon as you can. The current is already getting strong! I don't think I can bring her out of this! Let me know! Let me know!"

"Yes. I think we are committed!" Dave called back.

I tensed. This had all the makings of a disaster. Why was I attempting such an assaholic maneuver? Dave's eyes were glued to the water ahead.

"Ok. I think we're going to make it!" he cried. And with that we shot through the break, almost as if catapulted.

"Hard a-starboard!" he sang out as we cleared the rocks. Without the centerboard down, the boat slid sideways after my turn. I raced to the winch and lowered it as fast as I could. I moved quickly back to manage the tiller and the engine.

"We did it!" Dave called. "It's white sand as far as I can see!"

"Great! But let's not do that again anytime soon." I said, settling back. What I meant to say was *ever again*!

By about lunch time, we stopped on an unnamed island with pearl white sand stretching far into a perfect little bay. We swam for an hour, collecting an unbelievable selection of shells. It was several days later that we learned that sand sharks love spots like this but at the time, ignorance was bliss. We stored the shells in Pringles Potato Chip cans and threw over a few very old and now rancid sea fans from earlier treasure hunts.

There was no direct route between Double Breasted Cay and Grand Cay. A string of detached cays and small rocks, more or less awash most of the time, separate the two archipelagos. Our sail was in light winds and took us fairly far southwest at a modest 2½ knots. The chart suggested that we had Felix Cay on the starboard beam.

We sailed a course of 020 degrees, then dodged in and out of the channel cays. We accomplished all this by 3:00 p.m. before motoring up to the town dock. For the first time since West End, we were among land people. The local island boys immediately came down to the dock when we pulled up. As we tied off, I leaned over to Dave and said, "Is it safe to leave this boat here unguarded?"

"I don't know," he said "Let's offer to pay 'em."

"Ok, but they could steal several hundred dollars' worth of equipment by the time we get back," I whispered.

"True. Do you have a better plan?"

"No."

"Do you have $50?" Dave asked.

I rummaged around and found a few coins. Dave went on deck and called the boys around him.

"Any of you kids want to earn some money?"

Six hands shot into the air.

"Ok. I'll pay two of you to guard this boat until we get back. Can you handle it?"

The biggest kid assured us he could handle it, and after zipping up the cabin cover, we left with a few prayers on our lips.

The island was the pits. It was poor beyond belief with garbage everywhere. We eventually found a small bar and ordered two beers that cost us $4.00 each, more than a six pack. Needless to say, we ordered only one round. The bartender was a wealth of information and so, so friendly. But it was clear as we drank our one very expensive cold beer that this was not the place for us. We did learn it had been the hideaway for Robert Abpanalp, who owned the island, as well as his buddy, Richard Nixon. A huge white house on the other side of the island was where these heavies hung out.

With us drinking only one beer, the bartender got less talkative. We were concerned enough about the boat and decided to head back. We had not been gone for more than 40 minutes, but that's enough time for almost anything to happen. We quickly walked down the pier and there were all the kids just like we'd left them. The boat had not been touched.

Dave handed the big kid a dollar and was about to climb on board when the 'boss' announced that ice cream was $1.40. Could he please have another 40 cents? This was cheap enough and even though it looked like Dave was about ready to bargain, he thought better of the idea and just passed the kid the money. With the exchange complete, the kids were gone. We untied ourselves and motored to a quiet secluded cove for the night's shelter.

We arrived at Walkers Cay by 11:00 a.m. the next day. The course required a major detour around a sand bar, then a turn north passing Tea Table Cay. But coming up the long, well-marked channel to Walker's Cay Marina, we passed over a huge spotted ray heading south. It must have had a six-foot wing span and was perfectly visible in the four feet of the water. This was our second encounter with beautiful creatures of the deep and their impact on us was beyond words. This trip seemed to be a study in paradoxes. Things could be so beautiful and so frightening. Life in the sea was so picturesque and so ready to attack. The sea was so calm and serene one minute and trying to drown you the next. I wanted to see more of the beautiful side. I wanted to learn more about how to handle the boat and nature so I was not so vulnerable.

Walkers Cay was hard for us to believe. It was definitely for the rich. As we passed the little cabanas at the breakwater, we could tell this was going to be nice. And nice it was. Beautiful yachts everywhere, along with beautiful women, all attached to generally fat, apparently wealthy, men. The only flaw in the marina ambiance seemed to be us. A little yellow boat with two very poorly dressed sailors, was not a great source for community pride; we were clearly the poor cousin. The gas dock had never filled such small tanks, and the $25.00 a day fee for dockage was too expensive for our blood. We motored back out and planted the anchor on the sandy beach just outside the breakwater. We were alongside one other boat; a 26-foot twin keel sloop with three young college guys aboard. Within minutes we were swapping stories and sharing their cold beer.

Our chance meeting with these three was a stroke of good fortune. They were from Georgia and two of the three had spent a great deal of time boating. Although we had gained considerable confidence in the fine art of boat handling, we lacked the basics required to fish and survive off the sea. It was these new-found friends that created a "snorkeling for beginners" course designed specifically at our skill level; oceanic freshman. It began on the morning of the second day at Walkers Cay.

THE HUNTSMEN

    Using the more reliable diesel nestled in the bowels of our new friend's chartered boat, we motored a little more than a mile past Gully Rock and north. The chart indicated a substantial number of coral heads, just the place for a good day of snorkeling. Steve, the younger but more experienced member of the group, somehow felt we were in the right spot by about 10:30 a.m. and dropped the anchor. The bottom was at least 30-feet down so it was going to be long dive. To prepare, Steve applied a dash of Joy dishwashing detergent to our face masks to prevent fogging. He noted the importance of keeping one's facemask clear and Joy was the trick. With flippers on and spear guns in hand, all but one of us, rolled off the side. When diving, someone needs to act a backup and eyes. One person needs to be on the boat. Once in, a quick look around brought me the necessary orientation, then an almost breathtaking view of an underwater fairyland unfolded before me!

    I believe it was Jules Verne's Captain Nemo who once remarked to Professor Aronnax that the real beauty of the world begins at the shore line and moves out under the sea, not inland. It was certainly true at Walker's Cay. Once below the surface, rocky palaces tower above the sandy ocean floor. Countless beautifully colored fish swim lazily around these coral castles, eating algae from the rocks. Fish of every color, with no perception of man as a natural enemy, swam up to us quite tamely. The sea floor rose and fell around staghorn coral reefs, while patches of sea grass spread out like a lawn. There was the usual cacophony of popping and cracking and the random warm and cold water spots as we explored the world below.

This underwater Disneyland grabbed more of my attention than almost anything I had seen to date, but it was soon to be turned into a hunting ground.

At first, I was squeamish about taking my spear gun into this Garden of Eden to start blasting away at innocent fish. In fact, I was more than uncomfortable and Dave seemed downright annoyed. Both of us had been swimming around, just looking, repeatedly tapping each other on the shoulder to point out some new beauty. Now it was time for us to learn what we could and could not eat.

We learned that our goal was two basic types of fish. Fortunately, the less colorful ones were the eating variety. In fact, any brightly colored fish was off-limits. They make for poor eating, if not being downright poisonous. Well, that was fine. I just couldn't bring myself to sight some gorgeous parrot fish, aim my spear gun at it and pull the trigger.

The two types of fish we sought were groupers and hogfish. The first resembled a brown, blunt-nosed salmon; the other whitish and flatter, though they turned a reddish/pink when hit. Both were great eating, relatively slow and could be found under rocky overhangs, shallow caves and other such protected areas. The stalking process was the trick.

To arm the spear gun I had to put the butt of the gun into my gut, and pull the two rubber shock cords back, one at a time, into the dual catch. It was painful because the bands were so tough I felt like I was going to run the stock through my stomach before being locked in place. Once armed, and with the safety on, I took a deep breath and descended the thirty feet, blowing air out against my plugged nose to equalize the pressure of the water which rapidly builds up the deeper you go. I would then explore the underwater caverns upside down, with my head almost in the sand, to get the lowest possible perspective. Sure enough, I spotted a grouper. Because they depended on the color for camouflage they were slow to take flight. Whish! A reasonable kick from the gun and a thirty- inch spear was launched. The spear has a 6 foot cord attached so that you won't lose a spear with every shot. This meant that I had to be within at least five feet of my prey. A good shot was right behind the gills. Then you rapidly bring the speared fish to the surface so a trail of blood would not attract sharks.

Well, all this sounds simple, but my first six shots hit the rocks *behind* the fish. Since I was nervous and unsure of myself and had never killed anything in my life, it just was not a part of me yet. But, after two successes, the timidity and armchair morality disappeared. I became a "hunter" in the deep.

The first day I shot a grouper, two hogfish, and best of all—two crayfish (lobster to us Northerners)! I was exhausted after two hours of descending and ascending, reloading my spear gun and swimming around look for prey. Dave took over but since we had enough food for days, he had no interest in shooting more fish just for practice. There was no need for overkill. We simply wanted to eat, even though the fishing was good. We had no refrigerator and the extra fish would just go to waste.

Our three buddies were not of this persuasion. They would have shot every living creature out there, given enough time. Steve seemed to have no sense of limitation nor fear at all. He would be totally unconcerned about sticking his hand into a dark cave in the rock only to find a green, slimy eel. I was only too willing to give those ugly creatures plenty of room.

By early afternoon, we were back aboard and ready to have lunch. The fish were stowed in buckets of sea water to keep them fresh until we could clean them. Following a one-hour doze in the hot sun, we set out to clean everything while at anchor. For the next hour we had something of a small factory operating with each person stationed at various stages of the preparation. With the fish cleaned and divided among us, we cranked up the 'ol' diesel and motored easily back to the beach. The Nereus was bobbing casually at anchor, appearing glad for a day of rest. We beached Steve's boat, divided our spoils, boarded Nereus, stowed our new

Half-off Sail

food supplies, cleaned up, downed a quick drink and set off to the hotel for a chance to pick up any unattached female stragglers. And no great surprise, fishing turned out to be much easier.

The hotel at Walker's Cay is something special if you are coming from weeks at sea. I am sure it's super even if you are flying in from Fort Lauderdale, but it is something of an oasis after a long, hard sail. There was a pool, of all things, which we later used just to get clean. We used the facilities as if we were guests of the hotel. That meant ice for cocktails. No one complained. In the following days we sat by the pool and wrote sixteen overdue postcards. The luxury of it all was too much. Dave and I were glad to be back on the Nereus by nightfall. She was, after all, home. A small home, but home nonetheless. We prepared a feast. Three kinds of fish, with half a pound of butter, lemon juice from the bottle and the usual can of mixed veggies. The sunset was spectacular. Ice for our gin. Lobster, and two other fish for dinner, music, bobbing gently up and down in the Caribbean could only mean one thing: we were liv'in tall cotton .

At 8:00 p.m. one of the guys called over and asked us to come aboard for a drink. The tide was very low, so we just popped over the side and waded over to their boat. For hours we all sat around just bullshitting. It was easy to do because at about 10:00 p.m. someone brought out two joints.

Now, I can take or leave grass. Generally, I leave it. But this night seemed perfect for a hit and when I say "hit", Dave and I got knocked on our ass! I never had had such powerful stuff! Within five minutes, the starry sky looked like an explosion from Star Wars. The conversation grew very strange—each remark being totally unrelated to the last. The tide had dropped so much that the twin keeled boat was, or seemed to be, almost on its' stern pointed skyward. I was a mess and Dave was no better. By the time we understood the concept of going home, home was thirty feet away requiring us to wade up to our waist in emerald green water before we reached the bow. I went first, being as careful as I could to not get wetter than necessary. I lowered myself over the side into the bubbling, warm water, moonlight lighting up the fluorescent green liquid floor surrounded by a things sparkling everywhere.

I could hear Dave behind me. He was struggling to keep his balance, just as was I. Then—splash! I had walked straight into a hole. I could feel needlefish poking at my skin. Surely, there were sharks everywhere. And the water felt very funny. I could not wait to get out of there. Dave seemed equally anxious to get out of the water. I tried to change the racing conversation in my head, to think of something else, anything to get my mind off this liquid psychedelic torture swamp.

"What would you like for breakfast?" I said.

"For breakfast?" he answered after a very long pause.

"Yes, for breakfast. I'm sure something comes to mind."

More delay. "Well, yes." Dave said in a fog. "Now that you mentioned it, how about a bowl of roofing nails?"

My turn for a long pause, desperately trying to follow the conversation. "That sounds good to you right now?"

"Yeah, I'm serious, then a bowl of roofing nails."

"Ok, drop it. I'm sorry I brought it up."

We continued to wade through the warm soupy water, sure that fish were nibbling at us the whole way. I reached the boat first and tried to drag myself up over the side. My arms felt like lead, like they had been asleep and I couldn't get up over the side. Dave came alongside and seemed to be experiencing the same thing.

Here we were two hearty guys, in terrific physical condition, unable to get over the side of their own boat. It was ridiculous, and yet it took us whole minutes to find a way to figure out some method of throwing ourselves onboard. Dave tried to climb up the anchor chain, which caused the boat to nearly run him over. I just stood and stared at the side of the hull for a long time. I don't remember how we got aboard, just that we finally did. There had to be a lesson from this event, another teachable moment, but the only word that surfaced was abstinence.

The morning found us quite recovered, and we dined on lobster. In fact, we were to have lobster for breakfast, lunch and dinner for the next two days. Sounds like the height of luxury but if the truth be told, it got to be a bit much. We got so sick of lobster, believe it or not, that we spent $4.00 each to have hamburgers at the island weekly picnic on our final day. That was money we could barely afford to spend. Even while our taste for fish was a bit overworked, we could not get enough of snorkeling. We spent hours exploring the gardens below without a spear gun, enjoying every moment.

WALKERS CAY TO WESTEND

By July 4th, we began thinking about the long trek back home and spent the day preparing for our fast approaching departure. The knowledge that we would, once again, have to face the Gulf Stream had dampened many an evening's conversation. Now the time had come when we had to actually make the final assault. But before the battle began, we had the small task of getting from Walker's Cay back to West End.

We began that journey the morning of July 5th, only to be beaten back by choppy seas and a 30-knot head wind. After so many flawless days, we found it almost offensive that we would have such a struggle on our last day in the Bahamas. So with a mutual nod we headed back to shore where we spent the day in the hotel lobby, watching the wind gauge.

The next morning the wind had died out almost completely. This was no better for us than the day before since it meant that we would have to motor again. But we had to go, so motor we did. In fact, even when the wind finally did blow, Dave insisted we continue to motor. I agreed for a time, until I got almost paranoid. We desperately needed that engine to get us out of trouble in the Gulf Stream. Why use it now when every hour of extra usage made it that much less dependable? I became so obsessed with this concern that, at one point, became convinced Dave had lost all his marbles and was trying to kill us. My thoughts went, "Dave knows this is driving me nuts and is smiling the whole time. Now how is that for lifelong friendship? A couple of weeks at sea and *he* has become taunting, vindictive and mean. Me? Why I am just my same 'ole perfect self. How had Dave changed so much?" Camaraderie, like all relationships, boils down to a mind game. When you want to make it work, you find ways. You forgive or ignore everything offensive. If you don't, *everything* is offensive. I had to mentally pull myself back from the dark side and align with my buddy which, in time, I did.

The sails were raised at 11:00 a.m. Our trip was on a course of 227 degrees with a distance of about 50 miles, but with light winds it was going to be a long trip. Around 3:00, a squall marched across the water right toward us. We decided it would be a good time for lunch, so I took down the sails, threw out the anchor and enjoyed an hour lunch while the squall raged around us. Once it passed, we picked up the anchor, set the sails and continued on our merry little way. Shallow bottoms definitely offer advantages.

By 7:00 p.m. the lights of West End were in sight, but we had made an unpleasant discovery; we were off course to the south by a half-mile. This meant we were in very shallow water with a grassy bottom. In daylight this is not very difficult but at night we could not determine grass from rocks. Continuing on would have been extremely foolish so, within sight of West End, we simply threw out the anchor and copped out. God forbid anyone thought us to be foolish.

That night was one of the most unusual I have ever witnessed. The sky was still crystal clear at 9:30 then one of the brightest, loudest lightning storms occurred probably two miles away. The sound and light show was like some huge Hollywood production. And through the entire show not one drop of rain fell on us, the sky remained perfectly clear, while two miles away we watched the heavens speak their fury there was not so much as a ripple on the water. We sipped coffee and just watched in awe. When it was over, we applauded and turned in.

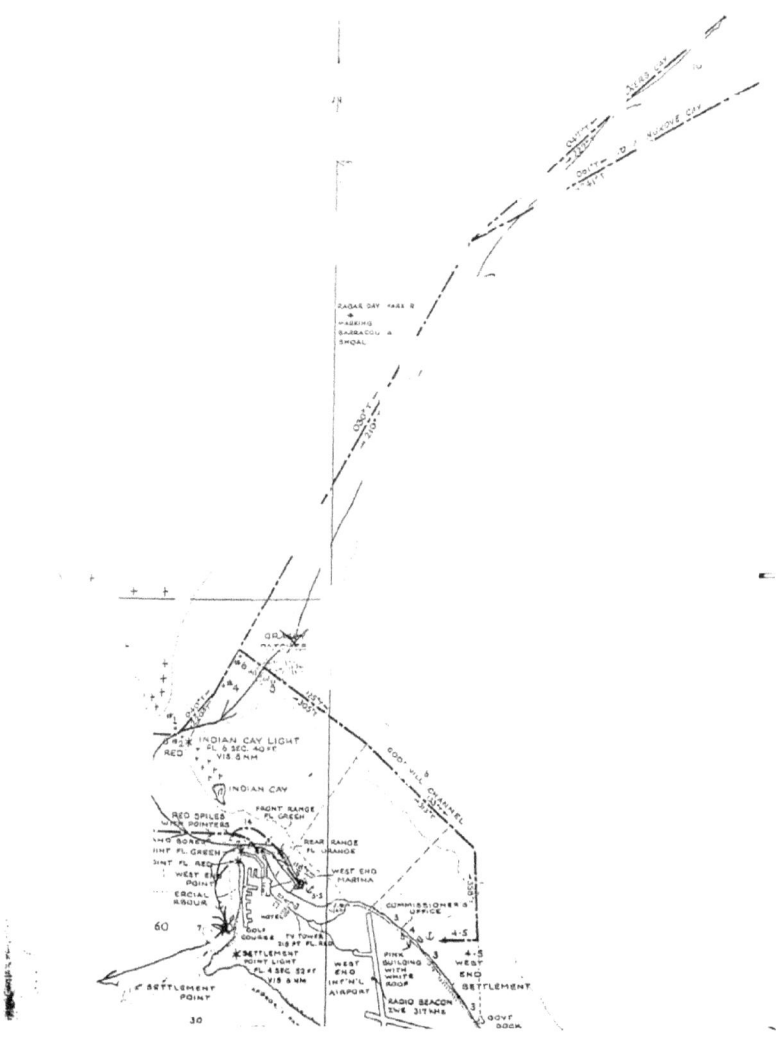

West End was a welcome sight the next morning, but the day there was spent preparing for the "final exam". We were both apprehensive since. This crossing would be difficult—there were no other islands this far north. If anything happened to the sails or engine, like the first time, we would just be swept away by the 4-knot gulf current.

We walked something like two miles to an Exxon station so I could get an extra spark plug. It was a fool's errand and a testimony to my temerity. The last problem that our engine would have is a fouled spark plug. But people love to pack mythical forms of protection against the unknown, and this was mine. A spark plug against the sea!

Dave was more practical. He found several plastic gallon jugs and once full of gas he spent the better part of the afternoon packing them safely under the seats in the cabin. We both felt like we were carrying bombs, imagining a hard-hitting wave slamming the boat down and cracking one of our precious little gasoline eggs. Gas running all over the hull in a storm would be deadly. But our choices were few and we did our best to carry the much-needed extra gas as safely as possible.

At 4:00 p.m. we motored out to Settlement Point and anchored with the intention of spending the night in a good spot for an early morning departure. Settlement Point was just outside the harbor, giving us a half hour head start.

Once anchored and cleaned up, I read for a while, and Dave went snorkeling to collect some last minute shells for his children. At one point I went in and scrubbed down the bottom of the Nereus to make her as clean as possible. When I got back on board, I casually looked over at Dave. He was immobile, face looking straight ahead at something under the water. I didn't think too much more about it until 15 minutes later when Dave was alongside asking me hurriedly to pull him up. I grabbed his arm and in one motion pulled him aboard.

"What's wrong?" I asked.

"I have had a barracuda this big," he paused to show me a four-foot long fish with both hands, "about three feet from me the last half hour. I just about shit when I first saw it and never was sure if it would attack or not."

Dave rested for a few minutes and then went below to start dinner. It was on the table without much effort by 7:00 p.m. and we ate in almost total silence. The fear from our earlier experiences had returned.

"What are you thinking?" I asked after a prolonged silence over coffee.

"I think we should set sail tonight," He said.

I nearly spilled my coffee as I stood up. "You what!?! I can't believe you said that!"

"Neither can I… but there's a breeze out there and it looks like a beautiful night."

I settled back down, took a thoughtful sip of coffee and said, "Ok. Let's go."

We were underway in twenty minutes. The sails were not set yet, but we were on course, powered by our trusty little engine. Just as Dave went forward to begin setting up, the engine coughed. I swung the tiller around so fast I nearly knocked Dave overboard. Already it was starting, I thought. We were only a mile out, but after motoring half-way back, we both decided the engine was fine.

"Maybe she just got some dirt in the line," Dave said. "Let's try it again."

I was not anxious to head back to shore and brought Nereus back on course for Pompano Beach, Florida. This was it. Us against the sea.

Dave set the sails, I shut down the engine and we started the shift. I went below to rest, but was wide-eyed listening to every revolution of the motor. Finally, I came back on deck and took the helm. It was a night I'll never forget. The sky was generally clear, so I aligned the mast with a star for guidance. Rather than continuously turn my flashlight on the compass, the star—at least for two hours—was the better choice. The full sails pulled like mules in the night. The sea hissed by. Pearl white foam curled up under the hull and spit past the rudder as we sailed on at four knots. The power of a sailing ship moving almost silently at sea, at night, is awesome. With our sails full, lines taut and a sturdy hull beneath us, a love of the sea and sailing fell on us like we had never felt. Here, on the last night, we had what we had sought for a year. Those hours captured what sailors have written about through the ages. Standing at the helm I was at peace.

By 11:00 p.m., I was tired. Dave came on deck and we changed positions again. The course was 220 degrees. Although Hillsborough Inlet was at 245 degrees, there was the Gulfstream always pushing us north. We were, as it felt from the stern, sailing almost straight south. But the run south close to the Brahma Shore gave us a better position when we hit the major Gulfstream flood some 30 miles closer to Florida.

We sailed on all night with ease. At one point, an engine could be heard in the distance. I turned a light on the sail to bring as much attention to us as possible. The ship passed in the night without incident.

We switched places again at 2:00 in the morning, then again at 4:00. With Dave on deck I retired below, crawled into the vee berth with a peaceful feeling and slept comfortably until 6:00 a.m.

"Bob!" I was on deck, through the front hatch, in two seconds, thinking, 'here we go again'. Even a good sleep was not too deep to hear Dave's call. Stumbling back to him I asked what the trouble was.

"Well, nothing yet, but I can see a squall coming and I want you ready to shorten the sail."

"At least we made it through the night in one piece," I said smiling. "How was the sunrise?"

"Spectacular!"

"Great!" I said, moving forward, "And, happy birthday! My present to you is getting home."

The squall hit at about 6:30 a.m. Dave didn't call for a sail change, and I spent most of the time in the passageway outside the cabin, holding down the blue canvas cover. The cover had always been too short, and with the wind blowing hard on it, the canvas billowed, leaving a two-foot gap ushering in gallons of rain water. There I crouched, holding down the cover against the rain, watching the sea ahead the morning of our last day at sea.

We had learned a great deal. Not only were we reasonably comfortable in the storm, but each move Dave made was perfect. Just as I thought he should push the tiller this way or that, he did. What telepathy! The boat was screaming along at six knots or so, in a relatively gentle sea. The wind was coming from the south which tended to flatten the waves. We were in a great shape. Now it should be about here that some disaster befell us. But, unlike nearly every other time in these situations, the sea gods smiled and said, "let them pass". By about 9:00 a.m. the ride was over, the storm abated, and we settled down to a more leisurely pace of two knots too leisurely against the Gulf Stream, so shortly I started the engine.

One of the problems of our sailing was not knowing our position. If there is nothing around, you just have to believe in your compass and keep heading in the right direction, even if your mind tries to convince you otherwise. Actually, you can sail for days with little concern for arrival, as long as you know where you are. But we didn't. We rarely knew our location, which is why we tended to panic when not sailing along at four to six knots. Slow speed meant being pushed around by the currents. Your mind plays games: "Yes, we are off the coast of Greenland...or Iceland or...

"Dave!" I called, snapping out of my fog, "Come here quick!"

Dave came bounding through the companionway and breathlessly asked the trouble.

With a squint and outstretched hand, I pointed to the coast. "Is that a building or a ship?"

"I can't believe we can see land this soon. I think it.. .well, let's check in twenty minutes."

Twenty minutes later, we rallied to have another look (actually, being at the tiller, I never stopped looking) and sure enough—they were buildings. We grabbed charts and description books and discovered we were right where we thought we should be. It was the checkered fuel tanks of West Palm Beach!

"Well, happy birthday to you, big buddy!" I bellowed.

We were both ecstatic! It seemed we were going to make it after all.

By noon we were motoring down the coast about 200 feet offshore. The good old Gulfstream had, even with a course correction and motoring, driven us about a mile north of the inlet.

We rounded the inlet buoy, plowed through the very choppy channel, knocked six ways to Sunday by a 60-foot power cruiser coming through at twenty knots, and finally, safety! We were back in the inland waterway.

We stopped for lunch near the spot we had lunched weeks before. We had about a day and a half of motoring to get to the car, which seemed like a walk in the park. We motored until 7:00 p.m., and tied up along a dock at an A & W root beer stand. And for the first time in six weeks, we made some telephone calls. We had forgotten how worried everyone was. What would you be thinking if you hadn't heard from two crazy amateur sailors for six weeks? Dead! Well, the reception was overwhelming. A bottle of wine with hamburgers and the works made a tasty dinner. It was over…almost.

The next day was uneventful. We anchored in some little cove and made the next morning's departure early so as to arrive at the car by around noon. Dave made a breakfast of leftovers while we were underway. The little-engine-that-could was doing fine.

"Which do you want: dried out nasty looking roast beef or greenish ham?"

"I'll take the ham," I replied. Five minutes after I finished, my peaceful world turned upside down. The dream had gone wrong, and so had my intestinal track. The little gas I thought I could pass unnoticed turned into an event of major embarrassment. It lasted right up to the public dock, which represented a bathroom rather than the end of a trip.

Once changed and feeling somewhat better, I returned to the boat.

"Did you make it?" Dave asked.

"Damn near."

"Feeling better?"

"Much!"

"Well, here's some news that will put you right back in the bathroom. The car is gone!"

I froze and my stomach did a flip flop. I looked around, and sure enough, the car was gone. An hour later, we had the story.

The officer that told me it was OK to leave the car didn't realize we meant three weeks. He had it towed away. The very guy that told me "ya, leave it" now was telling me with a smile that I was wrong.

A call to the garage revealed even worse news. The towing bill and storage fee would be $160. I could not believe the price. It was $80 for the car and another $80 for the trailer. Dave had $15 and I had $5. They would accept MasterCard. Only somewhat relieved, I hitch hiked the five miles to the garage, got there, found the car, gave them my card and it didn't clear. Talk about being pissed!! I was ready to kill. I had to hitch hike back to the boat and *we* had to come up with $160.

"I don't know where it's coming from." Dave said, completely discouraged.

"I don't either. Do you still have that sign that says: Lick you all over for 25cents?" I smirked.

Dave laughed until he cried. I just cried. After half an hour of racking our brains, I came up with an idea.

"I know a girl in New York whose best friend lives right here in town. Let me try and see if she's home and if she could call her friend and if her friend will loan us $160."

I thought about all the variables involved in this scheme and almost gave up. But the telephone call worked though unfortunately, Susan spent the first ten minutes screaming at me for not calling weeks ago to let her know I was alive. She'd been worried sick and seemed sure that if I did come back alive, we'd get engaged! I was far from such feelings and annoyed at the emotional discharge but grateful when she finally agreed to call her friend, Denise.

Denise drove up in a silver Mercedes 500 series fifteen minutes later, obviously able to lend us the money. Because it was Sunday, it was all in small bills and $25 in quarters. I kissed her feet and she even drove me back to the car with our battery tucked under my feet while making sure nothing touched the fine leather interior.

The front desk "legally-steal-your-car-and-put-it-in-our-yard-so-we-can-charge-you" person had changed, and when I described the car, she pulled out the slip with the trailer fines attached to it. For some blessed reason, she only added the bill up on the front page, which came to $80! Now, I am an ethical person and would not cheat someone with whom I had a legitimate debt, but I did this time and was proud of it. Those bastard thieves! I ran out of the office, dove into the car, popped the hood, jammed the battery back in place, hooked it up, started the engine, backed over to the trailer, hooked it up without lights and tore out of the lot. By 3:00 p.m. the boat was on the trailer, we were loaded and on the road heading for home.

Our money was so tight we ate Hostess Twinkies all the way home, but we couldn't have cared less. We had accomplished our dream and remained alive to tell the story. And, better still, Dave was one person I'd do it with all over again!

Not too many years later my wife Candy and our baby daughter Devon were at the tiller learning to sail the Nereus through the waters of the Peconic Bay in Long Island, New York. Funny how much that added to our life and set the stage for boating adventures in years to come. But, that is another story.

The End

ABOUT THE AUTHOR

If you like this book, you'll love Half-off Sail live! Robert (Bob) Fuller delivers wisdom and paths to problem solving through the experience of real life challenges.

Bob currently works with executives and organizational development teams in change management and productivity enhancement projects. Focusing on the balance between organizational and individual benefits, Bob has brought his own high level of expertise to presentations, coaching both teams and individuals, and workshops. His work, in such diverse industries as construction, health care, and alternative energy, has been key to the transformations sought by senior management.

Bob is sought after by organizations such as the American Management Association, Lee Hecht Harrison Executive Coaching & Training, Balancing Life's Issues Institute, and the International Center for Health for his uncanny ability to bring the human side of relationship and collaboration to teams tasked with left-brain driven projects. The result is the team's ability to quickly align and produce impactful innovative solutions.

Bob lives in Raleigh, NC with his wife in a historic more than 100 year old. He has rekindled his love of sailing and is in the midst of restoring another boat to share with his two daughters near the Outer Banks of North Carolina.

www.ingramcontent.com/pod-product-compliance
Lightning Source LLC
LaVergne TN
LVHW051835080426
835512LV00018B/2891